COLORADO CONCEALED HANDGUN PERMIT

(2nd Edition)

A reference guide intended for use with a professionally instructed Concealed Carry Class

By Timothy Hightshoe

WolfSinger Publications -- Security Colorado

Copyright © 2015 by Timothy Hightshoe

All rights reserved.
No part of this book may be used or reproduced in any manner whatsoever without the written permission of the copyright owner.
For permission requests, please contact WolfSinger Publications at editor@wolfsingerpubs.com

Cover art copyright © 2015 by WolfSinger Publications

ISBN 978-1-936099-14-6

Printed and bound in the United States of America

Introduction

Now, that you are taking the next step in getting your Concealed Handgun Permit, there are some things to consider:

1st — Carrying a weapon is a serious responsibility, and you need to be physically and mentally prepared. Keep in mind the first word, and the most important part of your permit is ***concealed***. You must insure when carrying a weapon that you are the only one who knows it is there.

2nd — All confrontations you are in include a deadly weapon— ***YOURS!*** If you are not able to defend the weapon do not draw it! There are times when it is far better to be a good witness than to intervene in a confrontation. Do not draw your weapon unless it is the only way to save someone's life.

3rd — Remember you are not a police officer; don't act like one. You are carrying a weapon to defend yourself and your family. You may also defend others, but be careful; you must be sure of the situation you are getting involved in. This book cannot cover all possible situations you may be exposed to; it is only an introduction to carrying a weapon. I would encourage you to seek more training, and to train on a regular basis. It is a good idea to shoot some form of proficiency course at least once a year, and maintain a record of your continuing training and qualifications.

4th — This book is intended as a reference guide to be used in conjunction with a class taught by a professional instructor, it is not a standalone course.

When carrying a weapon you should always have a cell phone and a spare magazine or speed loader. And remember something firearms instructor Massad Ayoob said: "The first person to call 911 is the victim."

Timothy Hightshoe

Safety

Before we start any class on the use of firearms. We must first gain a complete understanding of firearms safety. Most of us know we are safe with the firearms we handle, however accidents still happen every year. Most, if not all, accidents could have been avoided, or have not resulted in injury/death, if gun owners followed four basic safety laws. These laws apply in all places and all times to include the use of a firearm in self-defense.

1. All firearms must be treated as if they are loaded — ALWAYS.
2. Never let the muzzle of your weapon point at anything you do not wish to DESTROY.
3. Keep your finger off the trigger and out of the trigger guard until your sights are on target and you have decided to shoot.
4. Always be sure of your target and beyond.

Let's look at each of these laws and see how they apply to day-to-day activities.

1st - **All firearms must be treated as if they are loaded — always.** This eliminates the need for the excuse: "I didn't think it was loaded". Have you ever heard of someone shooting him or herself while cleaning their weapon? Normally they think the weapon is unloaded. This type of accident happens far too often. However, if everyone would follow this simple law we could almost eliminate accidents with injuries all together.

2nd - **Never let the muzzle of your weapon point at anything you do not wish to destroy.** This law is only common sense if you follow the first law. Do not point your weapon at anything you would not point a loaded weapon at. Again, this includes property and parts of your own body. This sounds easy, however it is one of the most violated laws.

3rd - **Keep your finger off the trigger and out of the trigger guard until your sights are on target and you are ready to shoot.** Think of this as the law of 'can', not the law of 'must'. Just because you have your sights on a target you 'can' put your finger on the trigger *only* if you have decided to shoot, if you are undecided if you are going shoot; **DO NOT PUT YOUR FINGER ON THE TRIGGER.** There are several reasons for this.

The first is called an inter-limb reaction. The brain sends a signal to one hand and the other hand receives it also. A second reason is postural disturbance; where you stumble, trip or are startled and your body tightens up. If your finger is on the trigger, you stand a good chance of an accidental discharge.

Remember you own the bullet and everything it touches from the time it leaves the barrel until it comes to final rest.

4th - **Be sure of your target and beyond.** This is extremely important. You can have a good center mass hit and the bullet may pass through the target and hit whatever is behind it. Even if the shooting is legally justified, if you hit a bystander in addition to the target, you are liable both criminally and civilly for their injury; this also includes property.

There are various weapons and types of ammunition that are prone to over-penetration. Make sure you know what you are using and what it will do.

In addition to the four basic laws, your instructor should have rules for class and range safety as well. You will notice most range and class rules are just an extension of the four laws tailored to the situation. This is a general list of basic classroom rules—individual instructors may have different rules.

1. No LIVE ammunition in the classroom.
2. No HORSEPLAY
3. Do not get ahead of the instructor.
4. Do not handle weapons until you are told to do so.
5. Personally inspect the magazine well and the chamber both physical and visually for ammunition.
6. You are responsible for your actions. You must insure you understand what you are doing and that it follows the four safety laws.

Basic Weapon's Nomenclature

Semi-Auto/Pistol

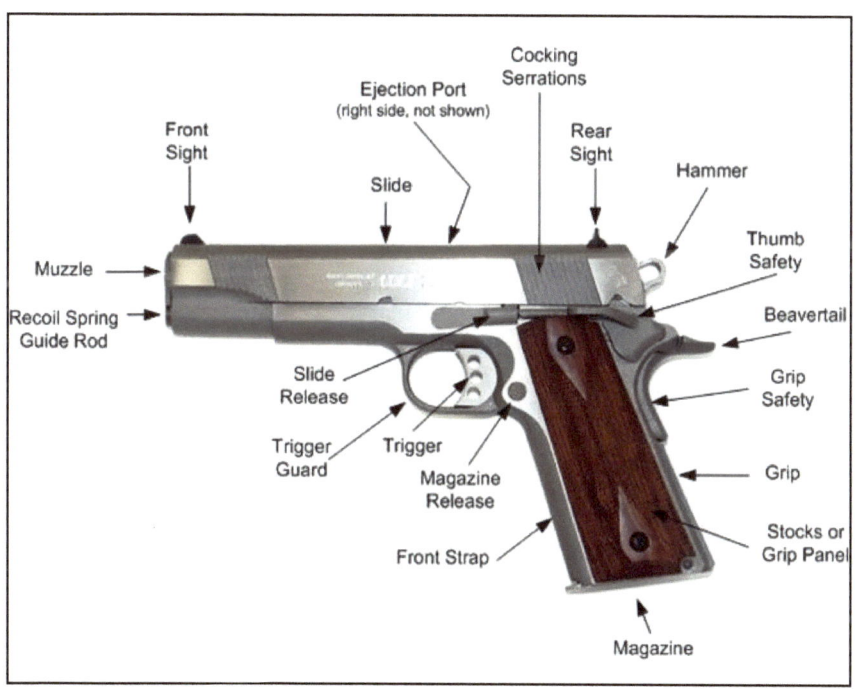

Revolver

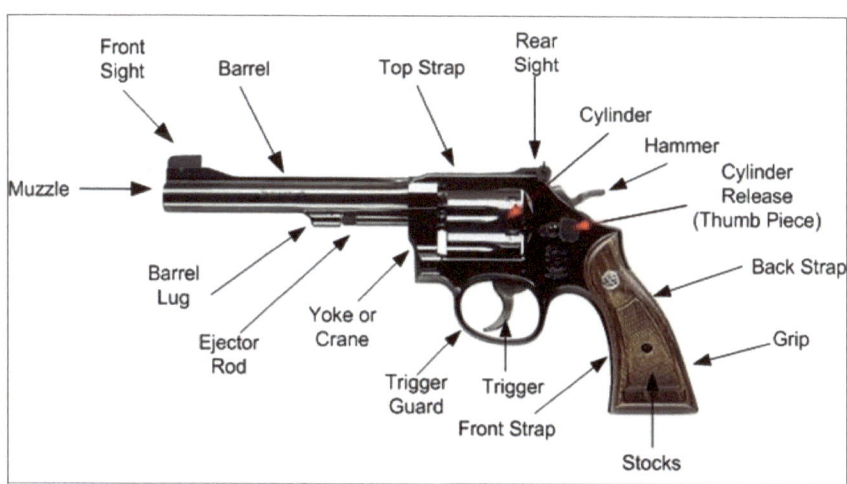

Cycle of Operation

There are nine steps in the cycle of operation of any modern firearm. Depending on the weapon the steps may be completed in a different order but all nine steps are completed for each round fired.

1. **Loading**: Placing a magazine in a pistol or placing rounds in the cylinder of a revolver.

2. **Cocking**: Accomplished by pulling the slide back on a pistol or by the trigger of a double action pistol or revolver, if there is an external hammer it can be manually cocked. Some weapons (Glock) have internal strikers instead of hammers but they work the same way.

3. **Feeding**: In a pistol feeding is accomplished as the slide moves forward pushing a round out of the magazine and up toward the chamber of the pistol. In a revolver feeding is the rotating of the cylinder of the weapon moving a live round into firing position.

4. **Chambering**: In a pistol the round is directed into the chamber by a feed ramp on at the bottom of the chamber (may be on the frame of the pistol or attached to the barrel). In a revolver it is the cylinder stopping at the proper alignment to the barrel.

5. **Locking**: There are many different locking systems for pistols, but all have some system of locking the breach closed preventing the gasses created from firing from escaping the chamber until the bullet has left the chamber area, some are as simple as the spring holding the chamber closed or as complicated as a falling or rotating locking block. For most revolvers locking is accomplished with a paw or pin extending from the frame of the weapon holding the cylinder in place.

6. **Firing**: For both pistols and revolvers this is accomplished by releasing the cocked hammer or striker allowing it to strike the primer of the round.

7. **Unlocking**: Simply moving the locking system allowing the weapon to cycle.
8. **Extracting**: Normally accomplished as the slide moves to the rear of the weapon. For most pistols there is an extractor claw on the slide holding the cartridge; pulling it from the chamber. However, some use the gas pressure to push the cartridge out of the chamber. For a revolver it is after the cylinder is opened and the extractor rod is pushed.
9. **Ejecting**: This is the final step with the spent casing being thrown from the weapon either mechanically of by hand.

Cycle of Operation

Loading

Ejecting   Cocking

Extracting   Feeding

Unlocking   Chambering

Firing   Locking

Types of Handguns

There are four basic types of firearms: Single shot, Repeating, Semi-automatic, and Automatic. In addition there are three types of actions: the Single Action (SA), Double Action (DA), and the Single Action/Double Action (SA/DA). All firearms fall into one of these categories. In this section, we will look at examples discuss advantages and disadvantages for each.

Single shot firearms are those that hold only one round, but may be of SA, DA, or SA/DA design. All single shot weapons must be loaded or reloaded for each shot. Some examples of single shot firearms are any muzzleloader, the Anchutz model 54 target rifle and the Ruger Model 1.

Repeating firearms are those that hold more than one round, but must be manually operated between shots to load the next round. This type of weapon may be of SA, DA, or SA/DA design. Some examples of repeating firearms are the Colt Single Action, the Winchester model 94, and many bolt action rifles.

Semi-automatic, also called semi-auto, firearms use the gas pressure or recoil generated during firing to cycle the action and load the next round. Even though the next round is loaded in the chamber, the trigger still has to be pressed to fire each shot. This type of firearm can use all three types of actions (SA, DA, or SA/DA). Some examples of semi-automatic weapons are the Colt 1911a1, Colt AR 15, and Beretta 92G.

Automatic weapons use the gas pressure or recoil generated during firing, and will continue to fire as long as the trigger is pressed and ammunition is present. Automatic is one of the most misused firearm terms. Many times when someone refers to an automatic firearm they are actually talking about a semi-automatic weapon. The media is especially bad for this misidentification of weapons.

Most automatic weapons are of SA design; however, there may be some DA designs. Some examples of automatic weapons are the Colt M16, the FN M60, and the FN M249.

Single Action firearms require the shooter to manually cock the weapon before firing and again before each shot.

Double Action firearms allow the shooter to press the trigger, which cocks and fires the weapon.

Single Action/Double Action firearms allow the shooter to either manually cock the hammer to reduce trigger pull or use the trigger to cock and fire the weapon.

Smith and Wesson Model 19

This is an example of a Single Action/Double Action Revolver. This revolver's cylinder swings out to allow loading and unloading of all six cartridges at the same time. The action allows the shooter to either manually cock the hammer for the single action mode or use the trigger to cock the hammer and fire with one press.

For many years this was the standard police service weapon, because of its reliability and ease of use and care. The only disadvantage to this type of weapon is the limited number of rounds in the cylinder—normally six. However this can be compensated for with good marksmanship.

Colt 1911a1

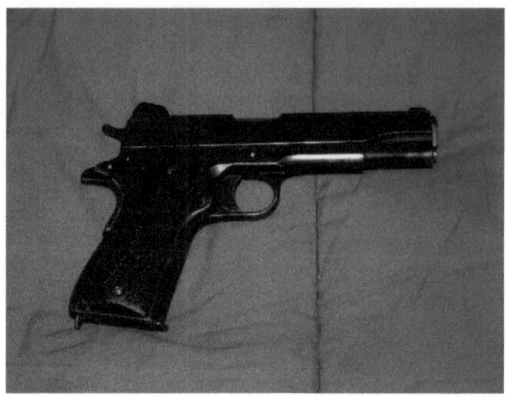

The Colt 1911a1 and its clones have dominated the self-defense and military markets for many years. This is a single action semi-automatic pistol. While it is normally chambered in .45 ACP it is available in several other calibers as well. It served the US Army for nearly 80 years as their standard sidearm, and is still favored by many shooters for its reliability and stopping power.

The magazine holds 7 or 8 rounds normally and can be replaced before it is empty allowing for tactical reloads. The disadvantages to this handgun are its size and some safety issues when carrying it 'locked and cocked'. This refers to when the pistol has a round in the chamber, the hammer is cocked and the safety is on. The safety system on this weapon blocks the trigger from being pressed, but does not prevent the firing pin from striking the primer of the cartridge in the chamber.

The 1911a1 has two safeties on the pistol; the first is a thumb-activated lever on the left side of the weapon, and a grip safety in the back strap of the grip. Both of these safeties block the trigger from being pressed. Some of the later 1911a1 style handguns do have firing pin blocks or additional safeties.

Walther PPK

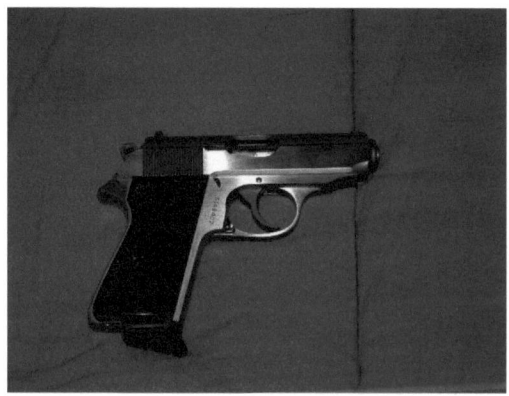

The Walther PPK (James Bond gun) is a SA/DA, .380 ACP (9mm Kurtz) pistol. This little gun is very comfortable to carry, though not as comfortable to shoot.

The biggest disadvantage to this gun as a self-defense weapon is the cartridge it fires. The .380 ACP is the smallest cartridge I would recommend for personal protection. What this gun lacks in punch is made up for in concealability, as this allows you to carry the pistol comfortably, which may mean you have it when you need it.

As with any self-defense weapon, it will not do you any good if you leave it at home or in your car. As with any pistol you will need to practice to have good marksmanship. This may prove uncomfortable to those with large hands, as the slide seems to bite a little. However, with practice this weapon proves very accurate.

Glock Model 22

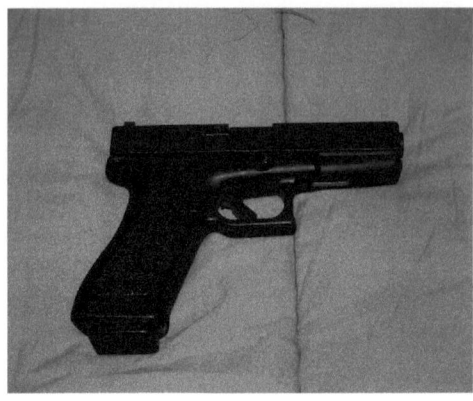

The Glock pistol is one of the newer weapons to enter the market. It is a double action only (safe action®) pistol. This weapon is rapidly becoming the standard pistol for law enforcement and security.

Available in several different calibers, although the .40 Smith and Wesson is the most common. The Glock pistol offers several advantages over other pistols. First is its weight; the pistol is made from a polymer compound with only the high wear parts made of steel. This reduces the weight of the pistol and allows for a more comfortable carry with a larger pistol. Although Glock introduced the polymer pistol, its success has spurred most major manufacturers to produce Glock clones.

Some other advantages to the Glock are the relative low maintenance. Due to the polymer frame there is little to no rust or corrosion problems. Glock produces full-size and compact models for most of the popular self-defense and law enforcement cartridges used today. Many of the compact models work well as backup guns for law enforcement officers, as they can use the magazines from their larger counterparts and they function exactly the same.

Now, that we have learned a little about the different types of firearms, let's look at which ones are best suited for self-defense and concealed carry. First, you need to evaluate your situation; are you in a high-risk position or just wanting a weapon to carry just in case.

If you are in the high-risk situation (law enforcement/ security, etc.) look at the type of weapon you carry on duty and get the same type of weapon system. This will reduce the risk of confusion during a high stress situation. If you do not carry a duty weapon, I recommend a full size duty-type weapon. What you lose in concealability you make up for in function. If you are looking for a just in case weapon, you can use a smaller and more concealable style weapon. Everyone's situation and reasons for carrying a weapon are different. Let's look at the main styles of handguns used.

Single Action/Double Action (SA/DA) Semi-Automatic

This is the most common pistol for duty or self-defense. The SA/DA pistol normally has more safety features than other older styles.

Single Action Semi-Auto (1911a1); this type of weapon offers some advantages in shooting such as a single trigger pull. Because of the length of time this weapon has been used, its main disadvantage is its 90-year-old safety system. The primary safety on most 1911 style pistols is a trigger block only. To carry this type of pistol safely, you need to either carry it without a round in the chamber or with a thumb strap between the hammer and the firing pin. Both types of carry can work well—if you practice.

Single Action/Double Action revolver: This is still a good concealed carry weapon, though some may consider it obsolete. Just remember, any gun will work as a self-defense weapon as long as it works every time. The revolver has some advantages in its simplicity of operation. Normally, there are no manual safeties to operate and no magazines to go bad.

There are some new 1911 style pistols with many new features; one good example is the Para Ordnance LDA pistol. Though they look like the venerable 1911, they are really double action only pistols. Again, everyone's situation is different and you need to evaluate your reasons for getting a concealed carry weapon. Look at when and where you intend to carry your weapon, the type of clothing you wear and whether you have to take your weapon on and off frequently.

Some of the features to look for in a carry pistol are:

1. Firing pin block
2. De-cocking system (SA/DA)
3. Trigger block safety
4. Comfortable magazine release/safety lever.

Size is another consideration: too small is uncomfortable to shoot, and too large is uncomfortable to carry.

Cleaning

There are too many different firearms on the market to write a blanket procedure for cleaning. However are there are some basics that are the same for all weapons:

1. **ENSURE THE WEAPON IS UNLOADED AND ALL MAGAZINES ARE EMPTY OF AMMUNITION.**
2. Remove all ammunition from the cleaning area.
3. Double check the chamber before disassembly of your weapon.
4. Use quality cleaning equipment and follow your weapon manufacturer's recommendation for cleaning and lubrication.
5. Clean your weapon after each use.
6. Clean your weapon weekly if you carry it daily.
7. Clean your weapon any time it had been exposed to bad weather (Rain, Snow, Sand, etc).

Storage

When weapons are not in use what is the best way to store them? This would seem to be an easy question but there are many variations of storage. New firearms are sold with trigger locks and to some this would seem to be the answer. However, it is one I don't like as most of the supplied trigger locks are grossly inadequate. They do not prevent the weapon from being fired if it is left loaded. Using a trigger lock on a loaded weapon is very dangerous.

Something to remember when looking at storing your weapon is most negligent discharges occur during loading and unloading. If you carry daily then loading and unloading increases the likelihood of an accident.

I recommend a lock box or safe the loaded weapon can be placed in. Still caution must be used when storing the weapon. Lock boxes come in many different configurations and varying costs. There are a number of purpose built lock boxes with different types of locking systems. Some have a push button entry system with a cutout of a hand on top so the box can be opened in the dark for home protection, while others use biometric (fingerprints) to open the box. This type of storage system can get costly, but usually starts around $100.00 depending on the type of locking system.

A more cost effective system is a fireproof box which can be purchased in most department store office supply sections. If you are using the fire box type of storage it is a good idea to put some closed cell foam or carpet in the box to protect the finish of your weapon. The drawback to this is most are opened with a key, which can be difficult if you are trying to get to your pistol at night without light.

No matter what storage system you decide to use it is important it prevent unauthorized access to your weapon, loaded or unloaded. If you use your handgun for home defense, you need to have a system you can access in total darkness under stress quickly. Practice getting to your firearm in realistic conditions (lights off) at night. You might want to also have a cell phone and flashlight near or in the box with your handgun.

Again every situation is different and you need to look at the environment (kids, other untrained visitors, etc) your weapon will be stored in and make choices from there, also check the local laws as some areas of the country have requirements for storage.

If you are going to unload your weapon for storage you will need a safe direction to point the weapon during unloading. There are a number of commercial clearing devices that work very well, but they can be cost prohibitive. Some simple and less costly solutions, are simply stacking (duck tapping) several old phone books together, and using that. How many phone books are needed? The answer to that question depends on the caliber of the weapon being cleared. A good rule of thumb is 6 to 8 inches of paper will stop most handgun rounds. If you have the resources to make a clearing stack then go to a range and insure it stops the round with at least 2 inches of paper left.

Another inexpensive clearing device is a coffee can or similar can of sand. Ensure the sand is clean and free of rocks. Playground sand is available at most home improvement stores for less than $5.00 per bag, and that is far more than needed. I experimented with this system and 6 inches of sand stopped up to a .44 magnum hand gun round. I also used an AR-15 with a 55 grain FMJ and that was stopped in the can. This is good for the one unintended round not for test firing a weapon. In the can the 4th round of 9mm penetrated the bottom of the can and was laying on the ground beneath. It took 6 rounds of .223 to penetrate the can. Additional protection can be gained by placing one or more layers of plywood beneath the clearing device. It is also helpful to have some type of aiming point in the center of the clearing area. The one I use is a coffee can with a smaller can inside. The area around the outside of the smaller can is filled with concrete, the smaller can is full of sand. I have tested this with one round from a 300WSM 180gr soft point round without penetration. Again if you have the resources test whatever you will use to insure it will stop what you are carrying.

The primary caution to using a clearing device—don't become complacent, safety is your responsibility and you must insure you do not have an accidental discharge even into a clearing device.

Sighting Systems

There are a number of aftermarket sighting systems available. Some will provide you a good sight picture in less than ideal lighting and some can slow down your ability to get a good sight picture. Before deciding to add any optional or aftermarket sighting system to your carry weapon do some research don't listen to a salesman selling the 'latest and greatest' sight. Below are a few general notes on the most common types of aftermarket sights.

Night Sights (tritium) are a common sight. It is normally a three dot system using phosphors with tritium to cause the phosphors to glow. Many manufacturers make this type of sight which can be very useful in low light shooting. The downside is it does not help in target identification. As these sights normally cost over $100.00 I recommend a good flashlight instead. If you can afford both then that's an even better idea.

Red Dot (reflex sight). There are several good red dot sights. Two major drawbacks to this type of sight are size and battery life. A red dot sight on a handgun with training can speed up your sight picture; but it must be practiced with regularly to remain proficient. Most mount high on top of the weapon and can be a challenge to carry and being an add-on any bump to the sight can affect its zero (alignment to point of impact of the round). Also this system requires batteries that can go out at the worst possible time. If you use a red dot system can you still use the weapon's other sights? Are you willing to trust your life to a battery?

Laser Sights. This sounds like a great solution to a nonexistent problem. However, they are one of the slowest sight systems to use and have the same problems as red dot sights. They also give your position away as a laser works both ways.

I have carried laser sights on submachine guns and some military weapons. On a sub-gun this sight works well for shooting from the hip or other unconventional positions.

The primary use on other weapons is to identify targets to others in your team. The primary one I used was an infrared laser—only visible to night vision.

One advantage to this system is an intimidation effect of putting the red dot on an aggressor's chest and telling him that is where the bullet will go through his body if he doesn't leave.

This may be valuable to Law Enforcement but as a Concealed Carry Permit holder you should never draw your weapon unless you actually need to use it.

Types of Carry

This section covers some of the more common methods of carrying a concealed handgun. We will not cover all conceivable types of carry; only the most common. Some holsters are inherently dangerous and we will not cover them. An example of a dangerous holster is 'Thunder Wear ®', an inside the pant holster that points the loaded weapon at your groin (Law 1). It is also very slow to deploy the weapon from this type of holster.

Hip Holster (Pancake)

The first carry we will look at is the 'Hip Holster'. There are several different styles of hip holster; some are better than others at concealment, however most offer good retention and a fast, smooth deployment of the weapon. This is considered an especially good option for law enforcement/security officers because it puts the concealed weapon in the same location as their duty weapon.

I prefer the pancake style hip holster. This type of holster normally has a thumb break retention device and holds the weapon securely to the hip giving it a low profile, which allows you to carry a larger handgun comfortably with fair concealment.

The holster should have some form of retention device; either internal or external, and should cover the entire trigger guard. Though not normally used for concealed carry, there are many other hip holsters available. The critical items for any holster are retention, safety, and comfort.

Drawing from the Hip Holster

I recommend a five step draw from a hip holster;

The first step is the grab or grasp of the holstered pistol. Depending on the type retention device (thumb break, role top, etc) release of the retention device is done in the same motion. Your support hand is brought up to the center of your chest at the same time; this is a defensive move as well as an aid to speed your draw. Your body moves faster if both hands are moving at the same time.

The second step is to pull the pistol up until the barrel clears the holster, then rotate the pistol until it points at the target. Once the weapon is pointed at the target this is the first time your finger can be placed on the trigger if it is appropriate to shoot (this is known as the close quarter's position and is used if the threat is in close proximity to the shooter).

The third step is the punch. Here you punch the muzzle of the pistol straight to the target; pretend you are driving the muzzle through the target.

The forth step is the smack. This is where the support hand meets with the weapon; it should be approximately where your hands clap during applause. Use caution to ensure your support hand is never in front of the muzzle of your pistol.

The fifth step is the presentation. Here your arms fully extend and you shift the focus of your eyes from the target to the front sight and establish a good sight picture. If you have made the decision to shoot, put your finger on the trigger and press if necessary.

Fanny Pack

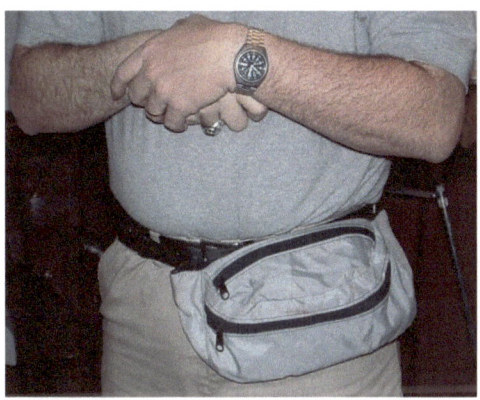

The next type of holster we will look at is the Fanny Pack Bag. Some of the advantages to this system include: being able to carry a large pistol or revolver comfortably, as well as being able to easily put on or take off without handling the weapon.

In addition to carrying a larger weapon, the bag also allows you to carry spare ammo and accessories (flashlight, handcuffs, small baton, etc). Some of the disadvantages; most people know what this type of holster is, and they will know you have a weapon. They may not know what type, but you're not really concealing much.

In addition to the lack of concealment, these holsters require a lot more training and practice to draw from quickly and safely.

Drawing from a Pack

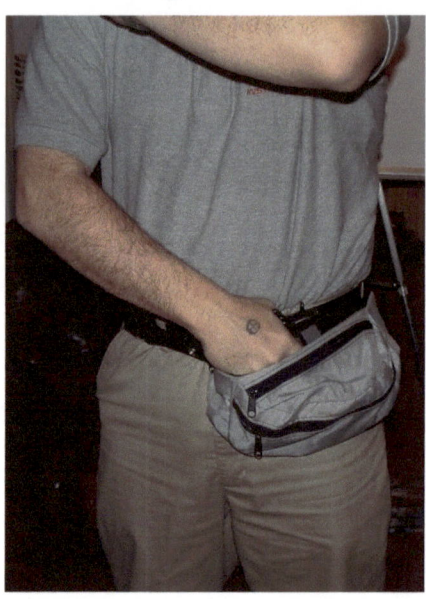

The first part of the draw is opening the pack's holster area, how this is done depends on the maker of your pack. Most use either zippers or Velcro® to hold the holster compartment closed. Depending on your particular bag you will need to adjust how you draw.

For most types simply grab the outer part of the bag and pull out or down exposing the grip of your weapon. MOVE YOUR SUPPORT HAND TO THE CENTER OF YOUR CHEST! Then establish a good firing grip on the weapon.

Draw the weapon out of the holster keeping the muzzle pointed down and use a bowling motion to bring the weapon on target. Your support hand meets with your firing hand approximately where you would clap your hands (do not allow your support hand to get in front of the weapons muzzle).

When placing the weapon back in the holster ensure you do not point the weapon at your support hand.

Inside Waist Band/Inside Pant (I.W.B./I.P.)

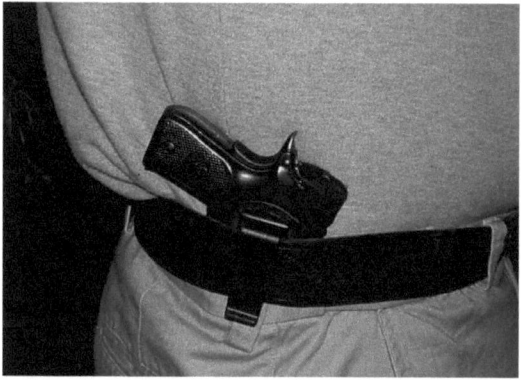

As you can see from the photo, this is one of the most concealable holsters on the market. They work very well for small semi-automatic pistols. As with pancake holsters, this style can be a good carry method for law enforcement/security officers as it is similar to their duty carry.

Some of the disadvantages include a lack of comfort with larger pistols or any revolvers. In addition to comfort, there are some safety problems with this carry. Holstering can be a problem as the holster closes when the weapon is drawn and you either need to use your support hand or point the loaded weapon at your hip to holster. Both of these problems can be compensated for with training.

Drawing from an I.W.B./I.P.

Drawing from an IP holster is almost the same as any other hip holster (See Hip holster).

The dangerous part to using an IP holster is in holstering a loaded weapon. A lot of shooters cant the muzzle of the weapon toward their hip as they holster (pointing a loaded weapon at their hip). This can be reduced by using an IP holster made of kydex® or other hardened material that does not close up when the weapon is drawn. The drawback to this type of holster is that the rigidity makes it uncomfortable for many shooters.

Shoulder Holster

The shoulder holster is one of, if not, the most common concealed carry method used today. Some reasons for the popularity of this carry include comfort, and concealability. In addition, it is easy and safe to put on and take off without handling the weapon.

The disadvantages include a slow and telegraphed draw. And, the draw can be dangerous if not trained properly and practiced. The disadvantages of a shoulder holster can be reduced with proper training and practice.

Drawing from a Shoulder Holster

There are two basic types of shoulder holsters: horizontal and vertical holster and the draw differs slightly for each.

First we will cover the horizontal holster.

The first step is to take your support arm and bring it up to shoulder height and cross body turning your hand so the palm faces out and place the thumb of the support hand in the crease between your arm and body. This creates what I call the survival pocket allowing you to draw your weapon without having your arm trapped next to your body, and without pointing your weapon at your support arm.

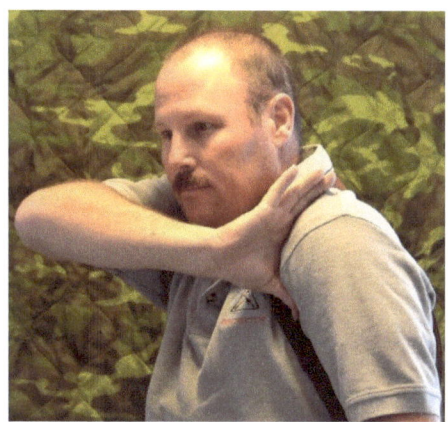

Then, your shooting hand establishes a good grip on the weapon and releases the retention device. Pull the weapon out of the holster and rotate the muzzle down then around to the front. This is basically a muzzle down ready position from here bring the weapon up to eye level and fire as necessary.

For a vertical holster everything is basically the same but you will need to pull the weapon up and out of the holster. If it is a front break rotate down and out of the holster and complete the draw the same as a vertical holster.

Important things to remember are to not sweep the muzzle of the weapon to the side, to put your support hand thumb in the pocket of your shoulder and keep your support arm up and behind the muzzle of the weapon throughout the draw.

Ankle Holster

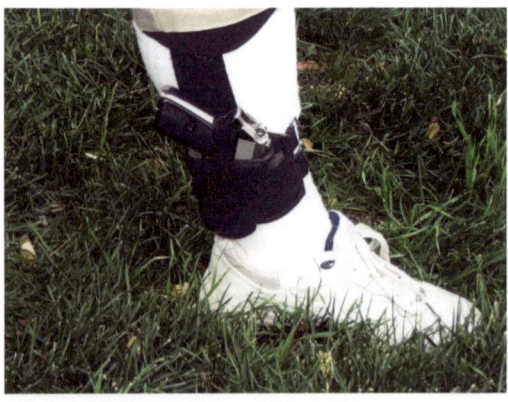

The ankle holster, though not as common as other types of carry, is used by a small percentage of people.

The primary advantage to this holster is concealment, as the majority of us do not look at someone's feet. This type of carry works well if you ride in a car a lot. However, it is slow to deploy your firearm; again you can improve with practice.

As with any holster system there are options to consider when choosing to use a holster type. The ankle holster can be worn on either leg both inside and outside depending on your preference and the situation you will be carrying in.

There are two primary carry positions: the classic—worn on the inside of the support leg ankle positioned just to the rear of the ball of the ankle the butt of the pistol toward the back of the calf. This position works very well for the person who drives a vehicle with an automatic transmission. When seated bring the support leg back to the seat and you have ready access to your weapon with little movement, though caution must be used to avoid pointing the weapon at yourself during the draw and presentation.

The primary disadvantage to this position is in a physical confrontation where the attacker may have knocked you to the ground and is sitting on top of you. In this position the pistol is not readily available to your strong hand and the retention system on the holster may make drawing the weapon with your support hand difficult.

A second position is on the inside of your strong leg, the pistol is carried butt forward and is again slightly behind the centerline of the leg. This position allows the weapon to be drawn even if there is an attacker sitting in your guard position. In addition to the availability to access your weapon in a ground fight, it allows your weapon to be drawn while seated at a desk or table without telegraphing the draw. While carrying on the strong leg may seem strange to someone who has carried an ankle holster, the strong leg carry is fast becoming my favorite ankle carry.

My primary use for an ankle holster is during classroom teaching, this position allows me to carry a weapon for protection of the students and weapons in my class. By carrying on the strong side it allows the weapon to be carried but requires a deliberate decision to draw the weapon while keeping it available if needed.

Drawing from an Ankle Holster

One of the first considerations for using an ankle holster is clothing, pants need to fit loose enough to slide over the weapon and be baggy enough as not to print (outline) the gun through the fabric. Other considerations are the length of the pant leg. Will it expose the weapon when you are sitting or walking? With that being said the pants need to be able to be quickly and smoothly pulled over your pistol.

Draws from the ankle are divided into three basic type:

1st is from a seated position: In this position raise the pant leg you have the weapon on using both hands—spread your fingers around your leg gripping as much of your pant leg as possible then pull your pant leg up as far as possible. Grasp the weapon releasing the retention device and bring weapon to the center of your body and punch straight to the target.

2nd is from a standing position: In this position you can bend at the waist and draw as if you were seated. This allows you to move and shoot. If mobility is not a concern or is not practical kneel on the side you are caring the weapon draw as before. The kneeling position is a more stable position allowing you to draw while keeping your attention on the threat.

Small of the Back (S.O.B.) Holster

This is a relatively new way of carrying a concealed handgun. Although it gives good concealment and security for the weapon, it has some major drawbacks. The weapon is placed in the small of the back right against your spine. For me this is uncomfortable when seated or driving. There is also a safety issue with having a chunk of metal or polymer against the spine. If you are knocked down or fall on it, there is a risk of spinal injury.

Lastly the weapon is difficult to access when seated. This is worse when driving; not only is your body against the weapon but the seatbelt is also in the way.

When choosing a small of the back holster pay attention to the direction of the weapon's grip—it should be up—not down. There are two reasons for this: First is concealment; if the grip is down this lowers the profile making it more difficult to conceal. Secondly, and more importantly, it is a safety issue. This position encourages an unsafe draw where the muzzle passes across the body instead of rotating around the body.

Drawing from a S.O.B. Holster

As with all draws, you will be faster if both hands are moving at the same time. Your support hand comes to the center of your chest as your firing hand moves to the grip of your weapon and releases the retention device. As you draw the weapon out rotate the muzzle down away from your body and rotate it at the hip.

Once at the hip, bring the muzzle level with the target and punch the weapon out, bringing it to eye level. Your support hand meets with the weapon in front of you approximately where you would clap. Caution must be used in the draw insuring your finger is not on the trigger until your sights are on the target and your support hand is never in front of the weapons muzzle.

Pocket Holster

Due to the increasingly popularity of very small "Pocket Pistols" (Ruger LCP, Glock 42, etc) the use of pocket holsters is growing. If you chose to use a pocket holster there are several considerations to its use.

Does the pocket you are carrying the weapon in violate Safety Law 2 by allowing the weapon to point at any part of your body?

I recommend the weapon be the only thing in that pocket. In a back or cargo pocket this is normally not a problem, but front pockets typically have keys, change, a pocket knife etc in them. Most of us have been putting these items in that pocket for many years and it take a concerted effort to change these habits. It is very easy to slip back into old habits when you are in a hurry or under stress and that can make a pocket carry dangerous.

Off Body Carry

This has always been an option for concealed carry; there are even some briefcases that will hold a weapon and allowing firing from them. While this is normally used for submachine guns they will work with semi-auto also. While this in not very practical for most people it does show the variety of carry methods available

Off Body Carry (OBC) for women who carry a purse can be one of the purses designed with a holster in it, although a specially made purse is not needed. One technique for using a purse not designed for a weapon is to use a pocket or IWB holster and place the weapon in a pocket inside the purse. If you want you can also glue or attach the hook side of Velcro® in the purse and get one of the holsters with the loop part of Velcro® on it. These holsters are commonly used in the 511 style jackets and vests.

Other OBC come in Day Planner types with one side set up to carry your pistol. Also there are several backpacks set up for carrying a pistol.

The two biggest concerns to an OBC is security of the weapon. This type of carry lends itself to the pistol being left unattended when you have to go to the restroom or are called away for something. Second when using an OBC system make sure you can quickly and safely draw the weapon if needed.

I personally do not recommend an OBC very often. Security is the primary reason as there are far too many purse snatchers out there and an OBC is a prime target. Many of the bad guys pay attention to concealed carry clothing and accessories making these prime targets if they can get their hands on them. If they are left in a vehicle it makes the vehicle a target to be broken into.

All in all the use of a OBC system needs to be looked at from a safety and security view then weigh the convenience of the system before you decide to use one.

Ammunition Types and Uses

What type of ammunition should I carry? This is a question that really does not have a single good answer, plus there is no one type of ammunition that works well in all locations or situations. A lot depends on your use and location. One general rule to follow is to avoid the hype. Someone is always making the ultimate bullet for self-defense, though most are just slight variations on traditional ammo.

In this section we will look at the most common bullets, and where they can be best used. Some bullets are good for target practice, and others are good for hunting or duty while others primary use seems to be in getting you sued.

We need to start by looking what makes up 'bullets'. First, the bullet is the projectile that leaves the weapon when it is fired — not the entire cartridge. The cartridge is made up of several components: Case, Primer, Powder, and the Bullet. We will look at each component individually.

Case: This is the base of all modern cartridges; it is usually made of brass, though other materials are sometimes used. There are several designs of casings illustrated below.

Primer: This is the part used to start the powder burning. It consists of a soft metal cup, explosive mix, and an anvil. When the hammer strikes the primer, the explosive mix is pinched between the cup and anvil causing it to explode and providing a spark or flame through the primer hole in the case, igniting the powder.

Powder: There are many types of powder used in modern cartridges; most are a smokeless nitrocellulose based product. Each powder burns at different rates and must match the weapon it is used in. This is done at the factory for commercially produced ammunition. A powder that burns too fast may produce a dangerous overpressure in the weapon when fired. It can also be just as dangerous to use a powder that is too slow.

This section will not go into reloading ammunition or powder selection; the information provided here is to allow a better understanding of how the cartridge works. This should allow you to decide on the best ammunition for your situation. It is best to use commercially produced ammunition for all self-defense work. The use of hand-loaded ammunition can increase your civil liability after a critical encounter.

Bullets are the single most important component of the ammunition you chose, and with factory ammo it is the only component you have a choice in. There are five basic types of bullets to choose from: Ball, Hollow Point, Wad Cutter, Frangible, and Fragmentary (Shot Shell).

Ball and Wad Cutter bullets are fine for target practice and some hunting, but are not good for self-defense or duty use. These bullets tend to over penetrate and do not transfer their energy to the target.

Frangible bullets are used primarily in target practice. These bullets are made from a powdery substance instead of lead and are pressured formed into a bullet that will turn back into powder on impact with a solid object. This type of round is often used on indoor ranges, to reduce the lead content of the range. Though this type of bullet can be very effective in stopping an assailant, it has some legal drawbacks. The round will break apart in the target, and transfer all of its energy to that target. The devastating effect of this may leave the user liable for excessive use of force both in civil and criminal actions.

Fragmentary rounds are bullets that either have mutable projectiles (Shotgun Shells) or are designed to break apart before impacting the target. This is one of the most dangerous bullets you can use. They are normally advertised as an ultra-lethal round. You should avoid any round that clams it is ultra-lethal. All bullets can be lethal when used and the ultra-lethal bullets will only get you sued if you have to use them.

The last bullet type is the hollow point. This is the primary round used in self-defense or in duty carry. This bullet type has a hollow cavity in the tip, which allows the bullet to expand when it hits a solid object. The expansion of the bullet will transfer the bullet's energy to the target and reduce over-penetration. This is the primary reason most law enforcement agencies carry these type of rounds.

In addition to the five types of bullets there are four basic construction types: Full Metal Jacket, Jacketed Hollow Point, Lead or Frangible, and Plated.

The Full Metal Jacket (FMJ) bullets have a copper jacket that covers most of the bullet. In some FMJ bullets, the base of the bullet may have exposed lead or core material.

Jacketed Hollow Points or Jacketed Soft Point rounds have a jacket that covers ½ to ¾ of the bullet and allows it to be fired at a higher velocity. The hollow point allows for expansion of the bullet and the jacket helps the round from breaking apart.

Lead or frangible bullets are cast or formed from a base component (Lead, Copper alloy, etc). The bullet is basically a ball type round, but may have a hollow point, or be scored to fragment. This is one of the oldest types of bullets.

Plated bullets are relatively new to the market, and are used primarily for target practice. The core material of the bullet is electroplated with copper or other jacketing material. The plating covers the entire bullet so no lead is exposed on any part of the bullet.

The following is from the National Rifle Association Law Enforcement Instructor Development School.

How Far Will It Go?

Caliber	Bullet Weight	Muzzle Velocity	Distance in Yards
.22 LR	40	1145	1950
.380 ACP	95	970	1089
.38 WC	148	700	1000
.38 SPL Ball	158	855	1800
.38 SPL JHP	110	1000	2300
.357 MAG	158	1430	2350
9mm Lugar	125	1140	1900
.40 S&W JHP	180	990	2000
10mm STHP	175	1125	1873
.44 MAG	240	1575	2500
.45 ACP	234	820	1640
.30-30 WIN	170	2200	3500
.30-06 BT	180	2700	5500
.223 BT SP	55	3240	3750
No. 9 Shot	0.75	1350	300
No. 4 Buck	20.6	1350	500
No. 00 Buck	53.8	1560	750
12 gauge Slug	437	1500	1500

Bullet weight is given in grains (in the case of shot 'Bullet Weight' is per pellet). Figures are from sea level; altitude increases the maximum range, as will tail winds. To convert yards to miles-divide by 1760.

CAUTION: These figures are intended as a guide only
Do not quote as exact.

Basic Marksmanship

Stance

The interview stance is the basic stance for all personal firearms' and weapons' deployment, and should be used in all unknown or higher risk contacts. This stance is designed to place the individual in a subtle defensive posture without appearing aggressive.

Start by positioning your feet and body at approximately a 45-degree angle, weapon side away from subject. Place your weak (reaction) side leg forward and your strong (weapon) side leg back. Your feet should be slightly more than shoulder width apart and your knees slightly bent. Bend forward at the waist placing your shoulders over the balls of your feet with your hips squarely over your ankles.

Avoid standing directly in front of the subject as this is a 'funnel' position which allows the subject to obtain a focal awareness point on you and places you at a severe disadvantage.

Grip

The grip on your pistol is one of the most important aspects of good marksmanship; it is the interface between your body and the weapon. Start by establishing a good grip with your strong (weapon) hand high on the stock of your pistol. This is more important with a semi-automatic pistol than with a revolver. A semi-automatic pistol's slide increases the muzzle rise during recoil and a high grip helps you control this effect while reducing the time needed to regain a good sight picture (discussed later). Though it is more important for a semi-automatic, this technique also works well for a revolver.

Along with the firing hand position, the position of the weak hand can greatly enhance your ability to control recoil and muzzle climb. Start by placing the index finger of your support hand against the trigger guard of the pistol and wrap your fingers around the grip and your shooting hand; griping with a firm handshake strength.

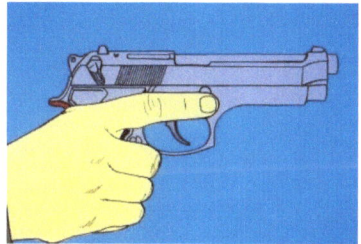 

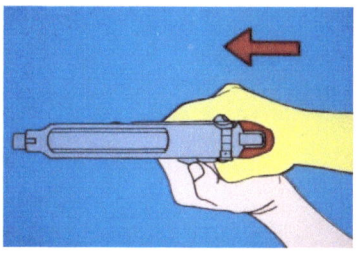

Use a loose grip with your firing hand. Approximately 70% of the grip comes from your support hand and 30% from the firing hand. This allows for more control of your trigger finger and better trigger control.

Sight Alignment/Sight Picture

Now that you have a good grip on your pistol, you need to aim it at the target.

There are two parts to aiming: sight alignment and sight picture. Sight alignment is simply aligning your eye, the sights, and target. Sight picture is what you actually see, when you look through the sights. The human eye can only focus on one object at a time, so what do we focus on?

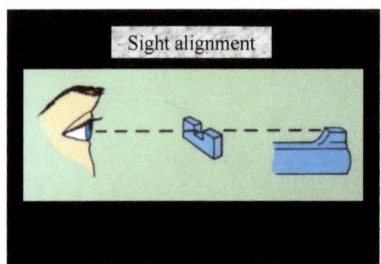
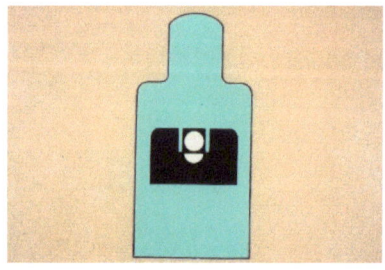

Try an experiment with an **UNLOADED** firearm. Pick a target 40 feet or more away in a safe direction with a good backstop, and sight on the target. With your focus on the target, your rear sight should be unusable and the front sight should be very blurry. Now, shift your focus to the front sight, the target will be slightly blurry, but still usable and the rear sight will be slightly out of focus but still should be able to be used. Lastly, shift your focus to the rear sight. At this point the target is almost gone and the front sight is blurry to the point of not being usable.

After performing this exercise, you should have noticed that you should focus on the front sight. This is the best for marksmanship, but may not always be practical in a tactical situation. Most people tend to focus on a weapon in the hands of an assailant; this is normal and at close range is usually not a problem.

The second type of sight picture is the 'flash sight picture', which is used at close range. You are focused on the target and bring the front sight up to your line of sight and fire using only the front sight and your eye as the rear sight. This method works well for very rapid deployment of a weapon at close (less than 10 yards) range.

Natural Point of Aim

The next element of marksmanship is natural point of aim. This is the natural centering of your body to allow your skeletal structure to hold your body and weapon on target with minimal effort. To establish a good natural point of aim start with a good grip and stance then bring your sights on target, close your eyes, take two or three deep breaths, open your eyes and sight again. If you are not on target, adjust your body so the sights lineup on the target, and try again. This procedure allows your body to work in a more natural and comfortable position.

Again, this is a good marksmanship technique, but is not practical in a tactical situation. However, if you practice this frequently, your body will learn where your natural point of aim is and adjust to it in most situations.

Breath Control

The next element in good marksmanship is breath control. Though it not as critical with a pistol as it is with a rifle, it can increase your accuracy. There are three primary types of breath control and although all three can be good, two require a great deal more practice to be consistent.

The first one we will look at is the top hold method. This is where you take in a lung full of air and hold it. This is one of the most difficult techniques, as it requires you to take in the same amount of air every time.

The second is the center hold technique. Here you take in a lung full of air and let out ½ of it. This can be very accurate with practice and it does not require you to hold a chest full of air and is therefore more comfortable.

The last technique is the bottom hold technique. Here you take a breath and let it out until it is comfortable—this is the lower respiratory pause. Your body is at its most comfortable, because you have exhaled all respiratory byproducts and you have oxygenated your blood. This allows you more time (3 to 5 seconds) to align the sights and press the trigger before having to take another breath. This technique requires less practice, and can be accomplished in most tactical situations. This is the recommended technique for practical shooting.

Trigger Control

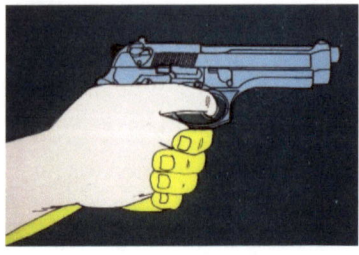

Trigger control is critical to maintaining consistent accuracy. Start by placing the first pad of your trigger finger in the center of the trigger. To find the first pad of your trigger finger look at the finger nail and draw a line around the finger from the back of the finger nail. Now place that line in the center of the trigger. When the sights are lined up and you are ready to fire, apply gentle pressure on the trigger pressing straight back until the weapon fires—you should be surprised when it does. This helps reduce anticipation and trigger mash.

Follow Through

The last part of marksmanship is follow-through. After the weapon has fired, continue to hold the trigger to the rear until the sights are back on target. Then slowly release the trigger until reset; in a semi-automatic this is a click that can be heard and felt. In most revolvers it is when all forward trigger movement has stopped.

DO NOT TAKE YOUR FINGER OFF THE TRIGGER UNTIL ALL SHOTS HAVE BEEN FIRED.

One-Handed Shooting

One of the most critical skills to be mastered could be one handed shooting. There are several reasons for this. Your support hand may be tied up using a cell phone calling 911, using a flash light to positively identifying your target and beyond, or it might have been injured.

To be able to shoot well with one hand we must first look at our grip. Because you only have one hand on the weapon you must have a good grip to be able to manage recoil while firing. You will need a high grip on the pistol if you are using a semi-automatic pistol. The web of your hand needs to be in the recoil shoulder of the grip on a revolver as high as possible without interfering with the hammer if it is exposed. After establishing a good grip ensure your support arm is cross body or in a flashlight position, don't let it hang at your side as this will unbalance you and make recoil management harder.

As you present the pistol allow your forearm to rotate slightly, no further than the 10:00 position for the right hand and the 2:00 for the left hand. This allows your forearm and elbow to work more naturally. When you throw a punch, to get maximum power, you rotate your wrist and forearm. The slight rotation when holding the pistol allows the same body mechanics to work giving you the best chance of managing recoil with one hand.

The rest of shooting one-handed is the same as two-handed shooting, trigger control and sight alignment are the same. As a note the weapon does not have to be straight up and down for proper sight alignment.

Reloads

One often overlooked aspect to carrying a weapon is reloading and immediate actions. Even though most self-defense shooting is less than three shots, it is important to be able to run your gun for a longer fight. There are two basic types of reload: tactical and combat, within these two types there are four primary techniques.

The combat reload is used any time you run out of ammunition. This requires immediate action on your part. The reality of a gunfight is—you will fire until you win or you are out of ammunition.

The next type of reload is a tactical reload. This is done when you win the fight or anytime there is a pause or lull in the fight. You will still have rounds left in your weapon and want to top it off.

We will look at each type of reload for both the semi-automatic and the revolver. The first step in any reload is to take cover before starting the reload. If possible never stay exposed to a threat target when reloading or clearing a malfunction.

Revolver Combat Reload: First open the cylinder and point the weapon up, with your weak hand holding the weapon open and the cylinder on your firing side.

With your strong hand, eject the spent casings with a sharp blow on the ejector rod. Rotate the muzzle to the ground, still with your weak hand holding the weapon and your strong hand retrieving your speed loader from the belt. Place the speed loader on the cylinder, release the rounds into the cylinder, close the weapon and bring the weapon back on target.

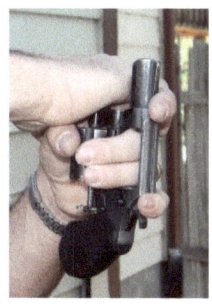  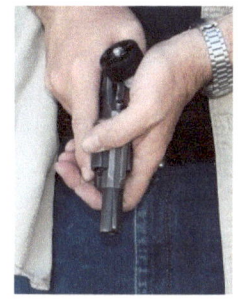

Revolver Tactical Reload: Basically the same as a combat but instead of dropping the expended casings and live rounds, you use the thumb of your support hand to eject the rounds into your strong hand and store them in a pocket.

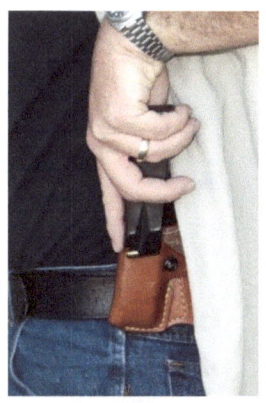

Semi-Automatic Combat Reload: First, your support hand goes to the magazine pouch and verifies you have a spare magazine and grasps it.

As soon as you have verified your magazine, your strong hand releases the spent magazine—let it fall to the ground. Your support hand brings the new magazine to the pistol, inserts it into the magazine well, and seats it firmly into the pistol.

There are several methods to close the slide. Most pistols have a slide release lever that will close the pistol. My preferred method is to grab the slide and rack it; this is easier to do, faster and is the same action used in loading, reloading and clearing malfunctions. As soon as the slide closes bring the weapon back on target.

Semi-Automatic Tactical Reload: When you verify and pull the magazine out, shift it between the index and middle finger and move it to the weapon. With your support hand and magazine under the weapon, eject the partial magazine and grasp it with your thumb and index finger, strip it out and insert the new magazine. Now, store the partial magazine in a pocket *not* back in the magazine pouch, only full magazines should be placed in the magazine pouch.

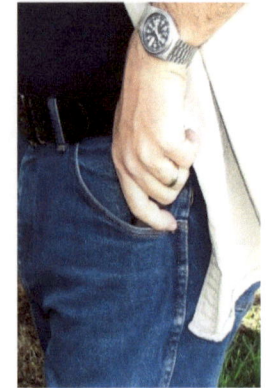

Immediate / Remedial Actions

There are two types of problems you may encounter in shooting: stoppages and malfunctions. A stoppage is any interruption in the cycle of operation of the weapon. They can be caused by the operator or by the weapon. Immediate action is the action to get the weapon back in service IMMEDIATELY. There is no attempt to identify the cause of the stoppage. Remedial actions are those actions intended to correct a problem. This is completed only if the immediate action fails to get the weapon back in service.

Immediate action with a revolver is simply pressing the trigger again. This will rotate the cylinder and bring a new round under the hammer—provided you have not fired all rounds. If you have, then perform a combat reload. Remedial action for a revolver is simply to perform a combat reload. If the problem still exists you probably will not be able to fix it at this time.

Semi-automatic immediate action: TAP, RACK, READY. **Tap** firmly up on the magazine in the weapon. This does two things: it ensures the magazine is fully seated in the weapon and may free rounds stuck in the magazine tube. Next, **rack** the slide of the weapon and allow it to close under full spring pressure. DO NOT RIDE THE SLIDE FORWARD! Finally, be **ready** to fire again if it is safe and appropriate. Remedial action for the semi-automatic pistol is to unload and cycle the action several times (generally at least three) to remove any ammunition from the chamber and reload with a fresh magazine.

Use of Light

There are many ways to use light. You may be using the light in the environment or providing light with a flashlight.

Always try to use available light to your advantage. In a hostile environment avoid being backlit (having a bright light behind you). Stay to the shadows as much as possible. If using a flashlight use it sparingly. Use it to navigate to a safe location, turn it on only long enough to see what is there, no more than 2 to 3 seconds, then move. Don't just flash the light, it will take you a couple of seconds to see what you have lit up and for it to register. If you are flashing your light, chances are you are telegraphing where you are going because you have to use it far more often.

Your flashlight can also allow you to identify your target, while at the same time providing you some concealment. If you have ever had a bright light shined in your eyes you know you cannot see past the light. This can give you a few seconds to move or engage the target as appropriate.

There are a number of different techniques when using a flashlight while shooting. You should be comfortable in several of these with the flashlight you decide to carry.

Flashlight Shooting Positions

There are too many variations of shooting with a flashlight to cover them all, here we will cover 5 flashlight positions as well as shooting with a weapon mounted light. Each position covered has both advantages and disadvantages. I recommend you become familiar with several positions. Some work well if you are using a cell phone and others work well while clearing a room.

Crossed

Crossed which has also been called the Harries position is one of the basic positions. Because of the isometric pressure of the hands it is almost as stable as a two-handed position but must be practiced.

As with any flashlight position caution must be used to ensure your support hand does not cross in front of the muzzle of your weapon. Also ensure your support forearm is not parallel to the ground this causes a shelf the blackstrap of pistol sits on. During recoil the weapon bounces against the wrist and can cause pain in the wrist. It also increases the muzzle flip because the pistol has a solid object (your wrist) to push against.

This technique is especially good for clearing around the right side of objects.

Uncrossed

In this position you press the knuckles of your support hand into the grip and under the thumb of your shooting hand. This position is a good complement to the crossed position, it allows clearing around the left side of objects.

Body Index

This position is also known as the neck index. I call it a body index because I normally use my cheek to index the flash light. The downside to this position is it requires one handed shooting. The upside is your weapon is not necessarily pointing where your flashlight is. This is good when you have an unknown threat. Also if you are not using a pistol with night sights this technique allows you to light up your sights giving you a better sight picture.

This is the primary flashlight position used by Law Enforcement during an initial stop or traffic stop where the weapon is normally in the holster.

This is also a good searching technique as it allows you to rapidly present your weapon if needed without pointing your weapon at something you do not plan on destroying.

Stacked

This position is more appropriate for use with a semi-automatic or a revolver with a flat bottom to the grip. This position allows the weapon to rest on the flashlight and keep the muzzle and flashlight pointing in the same direction. This is good if you have known threats in the area but not the preferred way to search for unknown threats. A second difficulty in using this technique comes during recoil. The energy from the round is transmitted through the backstrap of the weapon and causes more felt recoil and a separation of the weapon and flashlight. This takes more time for follow up shots. With this position you do not get the advantage of illuminating the sight of the weapon, but works well with a side button flashlight.

Wrapped Fingers

This technique is the closest to a two handed hold on the pistol. It is easiest to use a side button flashlight in this position. The flashlight is held by the thumb and index finger of the support hand and the body of the flashlight runs along the thump to the palm\wrist either the thumb or the index finger on the button. The remaining three fingers of the support hand are wrapped around the firing hand grip on the weapon. This position is one of the best for shooting from but has some disadvantages in tactics. This position takes the most time to establish the grip. In addition the flashlight is located on the support side of the weapon.

This position works well if you are going around a strong side barricade or wall but if going to the support side you must expose more of yourself before you can light up the area. Also the back splash of light if the wall or barricade is light color can temporarily blind you and destroy your night vision.

F.B.I.

This is the least useful of the basic positions. This position is a one handed shooting position with the flashlight held out from the body. The thought behind this is the "bad" guy will shoot at the light and miss you, the problem is with your support arm fully extended it makes holding your weapon steady more difficult, any movement of the light can transmit through your body and effect your shot.

The two primary advantages to this position are being able to light up an area beyond an object you are hiding behind and that your weapon is independent of the flashlight. This is important if you are searching for an unknown threat and encounter a non-threat (family member, house guest, etc.). You can keep your light on the area without covering people or things you are not willing to shoot.

Weapons Mounted Light

Use of weapon mounted lights has rapidly expanded from Law Enforcement and military to the private sector. There are a number of advantages to a weapon mounted light but there are some drawbacks as well.

The primary advantage to a weapon mounted light is you still shoot with a two handed grip on the weapon. The weapon and light are indexed together making for a more accurate shot. The problem in a defensive situation is the light used to identify the target is indexed with your weapon. This means you are pointing your weapons at things you have not yet identified and you have not decided to destroy. The safety issues with mounted lights can outweigh their usefulness for a civilian weapon.

If you have a weapon mounted light you should also have a hand held light to search with. This is extremely important if there are other family members in your house. The noise you heard at 3:00am could be your teenager sneaking in/out of the house, or it could be a house guest looking for snack. In either case you would not want to point your gun at them.

There are many different types' of switches for weapon's light so you must determine the best hand position for your type of light. Some things to consider, do not use your trigger finger to turn the light on, make sure you are not accidently pressing the trigger when you use the light. Insure your weapon functions properly with the light securely mounted. Some models of Glock and others tend to have stove pipe jams and failure to feed problems with a light mounted on them. It is more commonly the polymer framed weapons that have problems with the light attached. Polymer frames are designed to flex during recoil and a light tends to stiffen the frame and can cause timing issues.

Color Code of Awareness

The color code of awareness is shorthand for your level of awareness as you go about your day. Take time during your normal day to assess where you are on the chart and if you need to make adjustments to your mental state to be better prepared.

CONDITION WHITE
Relaxed state of mind, no true awareness of environment or other people.

CONDITION YELLOW:
Relaxed, but aware of environment and other people. Mentally prepared for possible trouble.

CONDITION ORANGE:
Someone looks suspicious or out of place and has caught your attention. Start thinking about cover, escape routes, weapons, hands, etc.

CONDITION RED:
Deadly threat identified. **MOVE** to cover, draw your weapon, issue verbal challenge if appropriate, and be prepared to fire.

CONDITION BLACK:
Deadly force confrontation. Fire until subject is no longer a threat. If subject gives up, order him prone with hands away from body and facing away from you.

After the threat(s) have been stopped, stay calm, stay behind or move to a position of cover, and call **911**.

When police arrive on scene, **FOLLOW THE OFFICER'S INSTRUCTIONS. IF POSSIBLE, HOLSTER YOUR WEAPON BEFORE POLICE ARRIVE.**

Tactical Considerations

There are a number of things to keep in mind when carrying a weapon, to include but not limited to: Who you are with (are they armed, are they trained and to what level), what are your capabilities (how far can you engage a moving target) what support equipment do you have with you (cell phone, flashlight, lesser lethal weapon) and your ability to leave or get away from a situation without having to use force.

Keep in mind why you carry a concealed weapon. Are you trying to be the 'Hero' and save the day or are you trying to give you and your family the best chance of surviving a lethal force encounter. I use the term survive because the best outcome *if* you have to use force is a still a rough one. You may have to put an end to a violent encounter and leave the aggressor dead or wounded. This is a good outcome but something you will have to live with. The best case is to use situational awareness and avoid a potentially lethal encounter if possible.

Because not all dangerous encounters can be avoided let's look at some variables you may have control over:

Are you alone? Is anyone with you armed and can you communicate with them? Know what resources you have around you. If it is a family member, do you know how proficient they are with the weapon they have? Do they carry a .380 (9mm Kurtz) with a 1 ½ inch barrel, or is it a Glock 22 with a tactical light? Have they trained to use the weapon with a cell phone in one hand calling 911 or a flash light in a darkened room or outside at night?

I would encourage a family that carries weapons to train together to be able to support and cover each other during withdrawal or attack as required.

During your training, push your limits. Try head shots at the range under limited stress and find your outer limit. Stress training can be accomplished by moderate acrobatic exercise (pushups, jumping jacks, running, etc.) to get your heart rate up and see how it affects your shooting ability. When doing stress exercises have a range officer monitor you. It is amazing how a rise in heart rate can limit your ability to see what is going on around you. Tunnel vision is one example of how stress can affect you.

After finding the maximum range you can achieve 100% hits cut that distance in half and that is the maximum distance you will be able to perform under the stress of a lethal encounter. Along with this you need to know the performance of your weapon's round against a human target. It is not like the movies. You won't hit an aggressor with a .22LR and make him fly backwards and disappear in a shower of sparks.

This book does not have the time or space to discuss the ballistics of all the rounds and calibers on the market today. I recommend you research the ballistics on the caliber and round you decide to carry. As I mentioned in the section on ammunition; some ammo is out there to get you sued. Don't buy into the hype and don't listen to a salesman whose job is selling the product that makes his company the most money.

Keeping in mind your abilities and your weapon's capabilities, look at the situation you are in: Is it a crowded restaurant or mall? How is the lighting? Can you be sure of the target? Is he the bad guy or an off duty cop trying to stop the same attack you are? Do you have cover or concealment? Is there a safe escape route? Do you really have to engage the threat?

If it is active shooter is there a pause in his firing to reload? Maybe this is the time to engage the threat but be careful; this is the time many bystanders will run and may be in your line of fire.

In the end everything boils down to situational awareness. Many bad situations can be avoided just by paying attention looking for those things out of place (trench coat in July). Trust your instincts; if it feels like things are going wrong leave. But not all situations can be avoided; give yourself the best possible odds. Look around; know where the nearest exit is. Look for cover and concealment in the area. Have a basic plan if things go bad. If you are with family do they know what to do? Talk about what could happen, have a plan to meet back at the car if it is safe. Know cell phone numbers—don't rely on speed dial. If something happens call a friend or family member not with you. Have a primary contact person for everyone in your family or group in case you are separated during a critical incident. This can help reduce confusion and aid in locating members of your family or group after an incident.

Stress and the Use of Force

This is a topic that can, and probably should take up several books if not more. There are many studies and a host of people who have spent their life researching this topic. I am not a psychologist or doctor; what I am including in this text is based on my experience and training. There are many sources to look at to get more information on the topic. Some books I recommend are: "On Killing" and "On Combat" by Lt. Col David Grosman as well as "Self Defense: When is it Worth it?" by Marc McYoung. As I mentioned I am not an expert on this subject; this is just a basic introduction to what you can expect in a lethal force or other critical incident.

What happens to us when faced with a life or death situation? I can't answer that question because each fight, each person and each time and incident occurs are different. Your actions will be based on several factors including: life experience, training, duration of training, length of time since training, sleep or lack of sleep, and any emotional baggage you carry. All of these can affect your response to stress.

Some of the more common reactions are tunnel vision, audio/visual exclusion, time distortion, memory loss. Some physiological responses are sweaty hands, nausea, involuntary defecation/urination, passing out, freezing or locking up. These are just some of the responses that commonly occur during a critical incident. Your response to a situation has many factors that can change. You might be a combat veteran from Vietnam, Iraq or Afghanistan but your response to a gun or knife being put in your face may be quite different if your wife and child are at your side verses being "in country". This is attributed a number of factors including mental preparedness. When on patrol or just in the hostile environment you have mentally prepared for a fight, but walking out of the mall talking to your wife and someone puts a gun in your face is a totally different situation. How will you respond, or will you?

There are several ways you can improve your ability to respond but there are other things you will have no control over. Memory lapses are common, you can only remember and report what you perceived during an incident. Due to tunnel vision you probably will not have any memory of what was going on in the background or around the incident. The mind is focused on the threat, but our peripheral vision will have seen parts of the incident you do not recall. This is why many of those involved in a self-defense shooting cannot accurately tell how many rounds they fired. Some memory of the event details may surface after 1 to 3 sleep cycles. This is due in part to the way the brain processes information. First, information is stored in the mid brain which is a kind of buffer system for short term memory. After a period of time normally 1 to 3 days (sleep cycles) the information is moved from the mid brain to the long term storage of the brain. PTSD is a failure of this function of memory and locks the information in a loop in the mid brain causing a person to relive the incident over and over (simplification of a complex disorder).

Some things you can do to improve your ability to respond is to run "mental movies". What do I mean by "mental movies"? It is a technique where you play a game in your mind of—what if. What if a person shoves a gun in your face? What if it is a knife? Run the variables: Am I alone? With my wife? With my kids? How close is he? etc. The brain does not know the difference between a mental movie and real life and this helps us deal with real life incidents as the brain thinks "I been here and done this before and won".

This brings us to one of the most important parts of your movie—always win. Always end with a positive result. Down side to mental movies is: the brain does not know the difference between the movie and real life and might add something to a incident that was not there, leading you to make a bad decision regarding the use of force.

Another technique is to practice combat or tactical breathing. One method this is accomplished by:

Breathe in through your nose to the count of four.
Hold your breath to the count of four.
Breathe out through your lips to the count of four.
Hold your breath to the count of four.
Repeat until you feel your body and mind relax.

This technique will help break up the tunnel vision and other effects of the situation allowing your brain to function easer. A critical part of this is increasing situational awareness which can reduce the surprise factor in an incident.

A game I play is the "Hands, Waist, Face" game. When you are walking around look at people: Where are their hands? What is in them? Look at their waist: Is there a weapon? A bulge under a shirt or jacket? What is the facial affect (expression)? Do they appeared scared, angry, happy or flat (no emotion)? The later for me is the most concerning. Being a people watcher helps with this game try to predict what someone will do in a given situation. Playing this type of game keeps your mind in the game and helps keep a good situational awareness, and that is the key to avoiding trouble or reducing the negative part of the startled reactions.

I am often asked how to prevent tunnel vision? I have to ask, why would you want to? It is part of what has allowed us to survive as a species for this long. Many of the reactions are positive reactions. Tunnel vision allows us to focus on what is important. Audio exclusion protects our hearing. All while ignoring that which we perceive will not kill us right now.

The important part is not to allow our base reactions to control the entire incident, but to allow higher thinking to control the outcome. This is accomplished by understanding, at least on a basic level, what we are going through and preparing before the event and our reaction. At Force Science they have developed many techniques for military and law enforcement personal to put our natural reactions to good use. There are several self-defense disciplines such as Tony Blauer's SPEAR (Spontaneous Protection Enabling Accelerated Response) System that incorporates the information from Force Science. Under the SPEAR system most self-defense actions begin with a "flinch response" simulating the body's natural response to danger and design the response from there.

Again, this is an introduction to stress reactions not a comprehensive course on them. The bottom line is we all respond differently to the situations we may find ourselves in. Not even experience will guarantee how you will respond. We can only do things to help improve our reactions.

Things we can do to improve our responses include studying what others have experienced. Running mental movies and trying to get stress inoculation through Reality Based Training or other stressed based experiences.

In the shooting environment, I like using shooting sports to give me some level of stress inoculation. Shooting IDPA or IPSC type shooting sports are a good start. Shooting a stage in front of not only the RSO and timer but a group of other shooters and spectators causes a lot of stress in most people and that is a good place to start. In addition to the stress inoculation it can be fun and help improve your shooting skills. Depending on the sport, it can also force you to practice shooting positions you are not comfortable with.

Some other effects of stress are what is sometimes called a central nervous system (CNS) dump: uncontrollable trembling or shaking, and a strong desire to talk. The latter is something you may want to avoid if possible. Having just experienced a major life changing event you might say things under the influence of that strong of emotion that can be used against you. Talking to the police shortly after a self-defense use of force may not be in your best interest. Remember the police are not necessarily there to help you, they are there to record as much information as they can including any statements you make under the influence of adrenaline and stress. Far too often in an effort to justify our actions we say things that can be easily turned around by a skilled lawyer. Thereby changing the meaning or making your actions look malicious. One of the best ways to mitigate this effect is to ask to speak to a lawyer before questioning. At this point the officer can still ask several questions you are required to answer, questions such as your name, address, where is the weapon(s), do you or anyone else need medical attrition. These questions are designed to make the area and you safe. What cannot be asked are questions regarding details of the event. By asking for an attorney or invoking your Miranda rights you allow yourself time to decompress and get better control of what you say. Even though you have asked to speak to a lawyer or invoked your right to remain silent you can initiate an interview with law enforcement at a time when you are in control of what you are saying. It is not going to help you if you refuse to corporate with the police at the scene of an incident. However, you need to be aware of the limitation and liabilities of offering too much information. Your actions may have been clearly justified in your mind and you will want to make sure everyone knows it. But, *and that's a big but*, talking too much will allow things you have said to be misrepresented by someone trying to dispute your actions during the incident. Also you will probably remember additional details of the incident after a day or two. If you have already said you did or did not see or hear something you remember later it creates a creditability issue with your statement. The only legal advice I give is—talk to a lawyer.

Given that you will talk to a lawyer, you must now choose one. Some things to consider: Is your lawyer familiar and experienced in defending self-defense cases? Marc McYoung pointed out to me one day that when you are claiming self-defense you have already admitted to the crime. If you had to use your CCW to defend yourself you have at a minimum committed felony menacing, all the way up to murder.

Wait what am I saying? You defended yourself right? What do I mean murder? CRS 18-3-102 says it is first degree murder if, "After deliberation and with the intent to cause the death of a person other than himself, he causes the death of that person or of another person". It can be argued that by carrying a weapon and drawing, aiming and pressing the trigger, you deliberately caused the injury to or death of your attacker. In normal court proceedings the state has the burden to prove you killed the person. But you just admitted you did; so their case is that much easier. Right?

A normal defense attorney only has to create reasonable doubt about your guilt in defending you. But in a self-defense case, he needs to prove the circumstances of the incident to prove your actions were reasonable and meet the definition of self-defense. Not all in the legal system are equally skilled at this. It is a good idea to have some help with deciding on a lawyer.

There are several originations who have insurance for self-defense (U.S. Concealed Carry Association, NRA, and others). These organization are able to help you find a good lawyer who is experienced at handling self-defense cases. I don't recommend a specific organization. Do your own research and find the one that best fits your needs. It is best if you do it before you need them.

Cover and Concealment

Cover

What is Cover? By definition it is an object that will stop direct or indirect rounds. What is cover really? It is anything you can hide behind that will give you protection. Cover is seldom perfect and it is dependent on the rounds being fired. The tire and engine block of most cars provide good protection against most handheld weapons. Although some ammo can punch through—especially in the rifle calibers.

Look at housing construction. Very little of a house can be considered cover. There is a small amount of protection from the 2x4 studs in the wall but this is not reliable and as I said—it is very small. Brick walls provide good cover, but be careful as appearances can be deceiving. Some houses have fake brick on the front that would not stop a handgun round let alone a rifle round. Our house was hit by a stray round several years ago. The round appeared to be a 9mm round fired at a street sign approximately a half mile away. The bullet went through the side of the house bounced off a kitchen wall went through a second dry wall and lodged in a 2x4—not much protection.

Bottom line is: don't believe the movies. Car doors will not stop a direct fired round.

Concealment

Concealment is anything that prevents you from being seen. It will not stop incoming rounds but is better than being a visible target. There is a story of a police shooting where a cop and bad guy were on opposite sides of a rose bush. Between the two shooters close to thirty rounds were fired and no one was hit. Each was trying to shoot over instead of shooting through the bush.

As responsible shooters we will always be sure of our target and beyond (Safety Law 4) but the bad guy may not. It is human nature to not shoot at things that cannot be seen or heard. If you do not have cover and are using concealment, noise must be kept to a minimum. As discussed in cover the walls of a house do not provide protection from fired rounds, but they do provide concealment. If you need to move down a hallway avoid rubbing or scraping the walls. The sound can give your position away and you can be shot through the wall.

Another form of concealment is light. If you can be in a dark spot and force the attacker into the light you will be able to see them without being seen yourself.

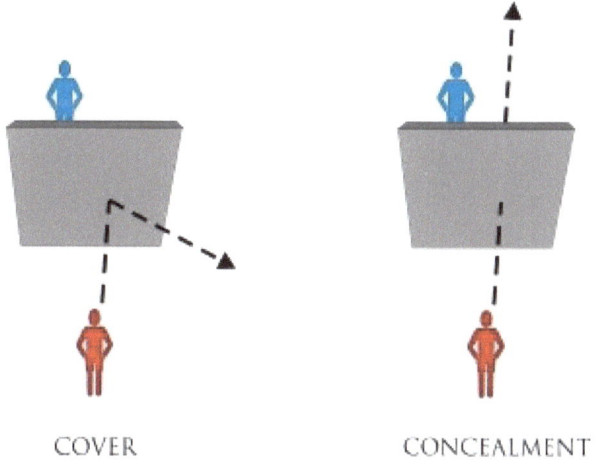

COVER   CONCEALMENT

Scan

One of the most overlooked and misunderstood elements of shooting is the post shooting scan. Often instructors tell students to complete a "scan" after shooting a string, though many do not explain what or why the scan is important or even what a scan includes. I often hear a scan is for more than one "bad guy", after all they do travel in packs, though this can be true it is only one part of the scan.

As mentioned about in the section on the effects of the stress of a self-defense shooting—tunnel vision, audio exclusion, etc. need to be broken up after a critical use of force and the scan with tactical breathing can help. But what is included in the "scan" and when should it be done. After all we have a known threat we should be watching—right?

Let's first talk about what a scan includes. Recently, I heard it explained as an evaluation of the tactical situation. The instructor emphasized the word as "eval eight sion" in reference to the eight questions to ask yourself during the scan.

1. Did I hit him/her?
2. Did it work?
3. Do they have any friends?
4. Do they have any family?
5. How's my position?
6. How's my weapon?
7. How am I?
8. How and where are my friends and family?

I know that's a lot to think about when you have just been in a fight for your life. That's the reason it needs to be ingrained in your training. During a training session, I try to ask myself each question after each string of fire before holstering. As we ask the question it becomes clear when we should complete our scan. If the answer to the first two questions is "no" go back and apply the appropriate amount of force and start again. Same applies if the next two are "yes". Remember to restart your scan with the first question after stopping to address any other issues that arise as you perform the scan.

The first four questions should get you thinking again and breaking up the tunnel vision that often occurs in lethal force encounters. The next four are questions to help you ensure you are in a good position.

1. Did I hit him/her? Use your eyes and ears to determine if you hit your target. Fire until you get good hits or the situation changes making shooting either unsafe or inappropriate.

2. Did it work? Follow the threat to the ground or follow (don't shoot) him running away—either one works. Remember you are using a weapon to defend yourself or others not to "kill" the bad guy. That might happen; but your goal should only be to stop the threatening behavior.

3. Does he have any friends? Look in front for anyone with the subject who would need to be addressed. This can be with your weapon or with your voice. Give orders to get on the ground. Place anyone who may be a threat in a position of disadvantage for your safety and theirs. Perform the friends scan out to 90 degrees from the front in each direction, remembering to look up and down depending on environment.

4. Does he have any family? This question should also prompt you to look around. Is someone coming up behind you? Remember to LOOK not just turn your head. It is common on firing ranges to see someone who is trying to do this turn their head just enough to see. This doesn't work during a stressful event as you will probably have tunnel vision. Glancing over your shoulder will provide you a glance at what is at your side not what is behind you. Also it takes a second or two for us to "see" what is there. Don't just **look** actually **see** what is there.

5. How's my position? Don't just ask yourself this. Act on it. If you are not in a position of cover or at least concealment move. Give yourself the chance to have the best outcome.

6. How's my weapon? As previously mentioned you probably will not remember how many rounds you fired. Break up your thoughts and check your weapon. Do you need to clear a stoppage? Should you do a reload (tactical or combat) as appropriate?

7. How am I? Our bodies and minds are incredible things. When confronted with the type of stress that occurs in a lethal encounter part of your brain shuts off. This accounts for the audio exclusion and tunnel vision. But, tunnel vision is not just vision—

it also includes tactile feelings and time perception. All of this allows us to focus on the what is important now (WIN) concept. The down side to WIN is it shuts down our ability to evaluate our own condition.

During a fight it is possible to be shot or injured without knowing it. From personal experience you can kneel on glass cutting your knee and not know it. This can also apply to more serious injuries. Often a person who was hit in a gun fight does not know they were hit until the fight was over. The good news is with current medical practices if you live long enough to know you were shot you will probably survive.

8. How are my friends and family? This part of the scan is started before the incident, discuses with your family or friends where to go during an incident. Some instructors talk about having a code word to put a plan into action. Have a meeting place selected (back at your car, nearest public restroom, etc.). Everyone should have memorized important phone numbers. Don't rely on your cell phone speed dial. Batteries die and phones break, get lost or taken as evidence. The plans you make should not be too complicated and code words if used (I prefer plane speech) should be something that will immediately put your plan in action.

This covers the family part but with our friends this includes the police call. Give them a good description of you, your family, and the "bad guy". Remember when they show up, no matter what you told them on the phone, you will be disarmed and handcuffed to make the situation safe for all involved. Don't take this as anything other than the police making the scene safe so they can sort things out. You will probably will be taken to the police station to be interviewed.

As part of planning how will your family get home? Who will take care of minor children? Trying to set this up when you are under the influence of the stress of a lethal force encounter is difficult at best. As part of your preplanning, spend some time with others who are often with you discussing these and any other issues you can think of.

Incorporate the scan as an active part of your training and ask yourself each of the questions before holstering. Develop good habits that will lead to success. Remember the saying "your performance will not raise to the level of the event, but will sink to the level of your training."

Use of Force

We have looked at different types of weapons and ammunition, now we need to look at when you are legally justified in using them.

Definitions

Before we can begin a discussion on the use of force, we must first develop a common vocabulary. In this section we will define the most commonly used terms in the UFM as currently defined by Colorado Revised Statutes, again you need to be familiar with the specifics of your location. By understanding the legal meanings of the terms listed here you will be better able to understand the UFM. In addition, a thorough understanding of these terms will aid you in applying the proper 'Balanced Force' in the performance of your duties.

BODILY INJURY: Physical pain, illness, or any impairment of physical or mental condition.

DEADLY PHYSICAL FORCE: 'Deadly force,' is defined as intentional use of force, which can cause death or serious bodily injury or which creates a degree of risk that a reasonable and prudent person would consider likely to cause death or serious bodily injury. It includes, but is not limited to, use of firearms, neck restraint, and intentional intervention with a vehicle (forcible stops or ramming).

DEADLY WEAPON: Any of the following, which in the manner it is used or intended to be used is capable of producing death or serious bodily injury: (I) a firearm, whether loaded or unloaded; (II) a knife; (III) a bludgeon: or (IV) any other weapon, device, instrument, material, or substance, whether animate or inanimate.

DE-ESCALATE: To use the least amount of force to stop the action of a subject and reduce the amount of force applied as the threat is neutralized or becomes compliant.

ELECTRONIC IMMOBILIZING DEVICE: (EID) Is a less than lethal, conducted energy weapon, that uses propelled wires, or direct contact, to conduct electronic energy to a remote target, thereby controlling and overriding the central nervous system of the body.

JEOPARDY: A hazard, a threat, or a peril.

IMMEDIATE THREAT: An immediate threat is considered to exist if the suspect has demonstrated actions that would lead one to reasonably believe they will continue to pose a threat of death or serious bodily injury if not apprehended without delay.

IMMINENT DANGER: Any action which leads to reasonable belief a suspect's actions would lead to the loss of human life. Or any action, which places a person in immediate threat of serious physical injury.

LETHAL WEAPON: Any object or material, when in the manner it is used or intended to be used, is capable of producing death or serious bodily injury.

LESS THAN LETHAL WEAPON: Any object or material, when in the manner it is used or intended to be used, is not likely to result in death or serious bodily injury. Any weapon, even those classified as less than lethal can be lethal if used improperly or in an inappropriate or unapproved manner. As unknown conditions (i.e.: heart conditions, asthma, allergies, drug or alcohol overdose) may also affect a subject resulting in death even with the appropriate use of a less than lethal weapon, the term 'lesser lethal' is becoming more common in reference to less than lethal weapons.

PHYSICAL OR NON-DEADLY FORCE: Any force, action, or weapon, which produces a result that is necessary to control the actions of another and does not involve the use of deadly physical force.

REASONABLE BELIEF: Having knowledge of facts, which, although not amounting to direct knowledge, would cause a reasonable person, knowing the same facts, to reasonably conclude the same thing.

SERIOUS BODILY INJURY: Bodily injury, which, either at the time of the actual injury or at a later time, involves a substantial risk of death, a substantial risk of serious permanent disfigurement, a substantial risk of protracted loss or impairment of the function of any part or organ of the body, or breaks, fractures, or burns of the second or third degree.

As a civilian with a concealed carry permit, you have to remember if you get involved in an incident in which you have your weapon, you have brought a deadly weapon into that incident and you must be able to justify your actions—usually based on the reasonable person assessment.

Unless there is an imminent threat to your life or someone's else's life, that cannot be prevented by removing yourself or the other person from the situation, it is usually best to leave your weapon holstered, take cover and be a good witness.

We do not advocate getting involved in every situation a robbery where the thief has a weapon, but has not taken a shot, may be better handled by standing back, letting the bad guy take the money or goods and being there to assist the police as a good witness. HOWEVER, if you can show imminent threat to life, such as the robber firing shots and you are in a position to defend yourself and others, WITHOUT putting others at risk, then you need to make a personal decision or whether to act or not.

To be prepared legally to make this decision, you should familiarize yourself with the statutes for the area in which you live: State, City, County, etc. and how they affect the carrying and use of a firearm. You should also be familiar with the legal definitions that affect the use of force as well as the use of a firearm.

Lastly, you will have to make the mental preparation needed to use force against another person.

Many people tell themselves they will not hesitate to shoot another person if they are defending themselves or their family. The truth is; that is a decision that cannot be truly made until you have actually drawn down on another human being and been put into a position to have to shoot that person, possibly taking their life. If you do have to draw your weapon on another person, DO NOT hesitate—odds are the bad guy won't. If you find yourself in that situation and start to question whether you can pull the trigger or not—DON'T draw your weapon.

Remember you do not go out and make the decision to use lethal force. If you are placed into a situation where you have to use your weapon, it was the bad guy who made the decision for you.

Post Shooting

Now what? You have just had the worst day of your life, someone just tried to kill you or someone you love. You used your weapon and won. You have called the police and they are on the way. You are still on the phone with 911 and you start shaking, you're scared and wondering what's next. You hear the sirens getting closer and then you hear. "DROP THE GUN."

You're first thought may be to look at who is yelling at you. Bad idea. You still have a gun in your hand. You don't want to drop your $1100.00 Kimber Custom Classic. Or do you? After all it could go off couldn't it? On top of that you don't want to damage your gun. So you start to lay it down and you hear. "DROP IT." Now what? I will tell you to drop it. Remember the first thing police will do is make the area safe for everyone.

At this point everyone is an "unknown threat" and you standing there with a gun in your hand are the focus of their attention. Some things to remember about dropping your weapon. You bought the Kimber because of quality and safety. It should not fire by dropping it. If you chose to buy the cheapest pistol from the back of a Chevy Impala on the bad side of town you might take more thought. Second, since you have used it in a shooting it will be going to the police evidence storage for the foreseeable future. Third, it will not matter how well you did during the incident if you get shot by responding officers.

All this comes back to training and during training you should be practicing a scan. As part of the scan you move to a position of advantage (cover\concealment). If you are in a good tactical position think about holstering the weapon before the police arrive. If not safe to holster put yourself in a position where you can safely ground the weapon without looking like you are pointing at the wrong person. Most importantly follow the officer's instruction to the letter. Even if you think they are wrong.

If the officer steps over the line there are avenues of addressing the issue without the use of a weapon. You will always lose an argument with the officer in the field. If you comply with his/her instructions, chances are you will not be injured and you will live to handle any compliant through proper channels: Internal Affairs, law suits, contacting the press etc.

Colorado Revised Statutes

(CRS)

The following is a list of the most pertinent statutes affecting the concealed carry of a weapon. Current CRS can be downloaded from the state website at no charge. It is highly recommended you review CRS each year to insure you are aware of all changes.

13-14-105.5. Civil protection orders - prohibition on possessing or purchasing a firearm

(1) If the court subjects a person to a civil protection order pursuant to a provision of this article and the protection order qualifies as an order described in 18 U.S.C. sec. 922 (d) (8) or (g) (8), the court, as part of such order:

(a) Shall order the person to:

(I) Refrain from possessing or purchasing any firearm or ammunition for the duration of the order; and

(II) Relinquish, for the duration of the order, any firearm or ammunition in the respondent's immediate possession or control or subject to the respondent's immediate possession or control; and

(b) May require that before the person is released from custody on bond, the person shall relinquish, for the duration of the order, any firearm or ammunition in the person's immediate possession or control or subject to the person's immediate possession or control.

(2) (a) Except as described in paragraph (b) of this subsection (2), upon issuance of an order pursuant to subsection (1) of this section, the respondent shall relinquish any firearm or ammunition:

(I) Not more than twenty-four hours after being served with the order in open court; or

(II) Not more than forty-eight hours after being served with the order outside of the court.

(b) A court may allow a respondent up to seventy-two hours to relinquish a firearm or up to five days to relinquish ammunition pursuant to paragraph (a) of this subsection (2) if the respondent demonstrates to the satisfaction of the court that he or she is unable to comply within the time frame set forth in said subsection (2).

(c) To satisfy the requirement in paragraph (a) of this subsection (2), the respondent may:

(I) Sell or transfer possession of the firearm or ammunition to a federally licensed firearms dealer described in 18 U.S.C. sec. 923, as amended; except that this provision shall not be interpreted to require any federally licensed firearms dealer to purchase or accept possession of any firearm or ammunition;

(II) Arrange for the storage of the firearm or ammunition by a law enforcement agency; except that this provision shall not be interpreted to require any law enforcement agency to provide storage of firearms or ammunition for any person; or

(III) Sell or otherwise transfer the firearm or ammunition to a private party who may legally possess the firearm or ammunition; except that a person who sells or transfers a firearm pursuant to this subparagraph (III) shall satisfy all of the provisions of <u>section 18-12-112, C.R.S.</u>, concerning private firearms transfers, including but not limited to the performance of a criminal background check of the transferee.

(3) If a respondent is unable to satisfy the provisions of subsection (2) of this section because he or she is incarcerated or otherwise held in the custody of a law enforcement agency, the court shall require the respondent to satisfy such provisions not more than twenty-four hours after his or her release from incarceration or custody or be held in contempt of court. Notwithstanding any provision of this subsection (3), the court may, in its discretion, require the respondent to relinquish any firearm or ammunition in the respondent's immediate possession or control or subject to the respondent's immediate possession or control before the end of the respondent's incarceration. In such a case, a respondent's failure to relinquish a firearm or ammunition as required shall constitute contempt of court.

(4) A federally licensed firearms dealer who takes possession of a firearm or ammunition pursuant to this section shall issue a receipt to the respondent at the time of relinquishment. The federally licensed firearms dealer shall not return the firearm or ammunition to the respondent unless the dealer:

(a) Contacts the bureau to request that a background check of the respondent be performed; and

(b) Obtains approval of the transfer from the bureau after the performance of the background check.

(5) A local law enforcement agency may elect to store firearms or ammunition for persons pursuant to this section. If an agency so elects:

(a) The agency may charge a fee for such storage, the amount of which shall not exceed the direct and indirect costs incurred by the agency in providing such storage;

(b) The agency may establish policies for disposal of abandoned or stolen firearms or ammunition; and

(c) The agency shall issue a receipt to each respondent at the time the respondent relinquishes possession of a firearm or ammunition.

(6) If a local law enforcement agency elects to store firearms or ammunition for a person pursuant to this section, the law enforcement agency shall not return the firearm or ammunition to the respondent unless the agency:

(a) Contacts the bureau to request that a background check of the respondent be performed; and

(b) Obtains approval of the transfer from the bureau after the performance of the background check.

(7) (a) A law enforcement agency that elects to store a firearm or ammunition for a person pursuant to this section may elect to cease storing the firearm or ammunition. A law enforcement agency that elects to cease storing a firearm or ammunition for a person shall notify the person of such decision and request that the person immediately make arrangements for the transfer of the possession of the firearm or ammunition to the person or, if the person is prohibited from possessing a firearm, to another person

who is legally permitted to possess a firearm.

(b) If a law enforcement agency elects to cease storing a firearm or ammunition for a person and notifies the person as described in paragraph (a) of this subsection (7), the law enforcement agency may dispose of the firearm or ammunition if the person fails to make arrangements for the transfer of the firearm or ammunition and complete said transfer within ninety days of receiving such notification.

(8) If a respondent sells or otherwise transfers a firearm or ammunition to a private party who may legally possess the firearm or ammunition, as described in subparagraph (III) of paragraph (c) of subsection (2) of this section, the respondent shall acquire:

(a) From the transferee, a written receipt acknowledging the transfer, which receipt shall be dated and signed by the respondent and the transferee; and

(b) From the licensed gun dealer who requests from the bureau a background check of the transferee, as described in section 18-12-112, C.R.S., a written statement of the results of the background check.

(9) (a) Not more than three business days after the relinquishment, the respondent shall file a copy of the receipt issued pursuant to subsection (4), (5), or (8) of this section, and, if applicable, the written statement of the results of a background check performed on the respondent, as described in paragraph (b) of subsection (8) of this section, with the court as proof of the relinquishment. If a respondent fails to timely file a receipt or written statement as described in this subsection (9):

(I) The failure constitutes a violation of the protection order pursuant to section 18-6-803.5 (1) (c), C.R.S.; and

(II) The court shall issue a warrant for the respondent's arrest.

(b) In any subsequent prosecution for a violation of a protection order described in this subsection (9), the court shall take judicial notice of the defendant's failure to file a receipt or written statement, which will constitute prima facie evidence of a violation of the protection order pursuant to section 18-6-803.5 (1) (c), C.R.S., and testimony of the clerk of the court or his or her deputy is not required.

(10) Nothing in this section shall be construed to limit a respondent's right to petition the court for dismissal of a protection order.

(11) A person subject to a civil protection order issued pursuant to section 13-14-104.5 (1) (a) who possesses or attempts to purchase or receive a firearm or ammunition while the protection order is in effect violates the order pursuant to section 18-6-803.5 (1) (c), C.R.S.

(12) (a) A law enforcement agency that elects in good faith to not store a firearm or ammunition for a person pursuant to subparagraph (II) of paragraph (c) of subsection (2) of this section shall not be held criminally or civilly liable for such election not to act.

(b) A law enforcement agency that returns possession of a firearm or ammunition to a person in good faith as permitted by subsection (6) of this section shall not be held criminally or civilly liable for such action.

16-3-201. Arrest by a private person.

A person who is not a peace officer may arrest another person when any crime has been or is being committed by the arrested person in the presence of the person making the arrest.

18-1-704. Use of physical force in defense of a person.

(1) Except as provided in subsections (2) and (3) of this section, a person is justified in using physical force upon another person in order to defend himself or a third person from what he reasonably believes to be the use or imminent use of unlawful physical force by that other person, and he may use a degree of force which he reasonably believes to be necessary for that purpose.

(2) Deadly physical force may be used only if a person reasonably believes a lesser degree of force is inadequate and:

(a) The actor has reasonable ground to believe, and does believe, that he or another person is in imminent danger of being killed or of receiving great bodily injury; or

(b) The other person is using or reasonably appears about to use physical force against an occupant of a dwelling or business establishment while committing or attempting to commit burglary as defined in sections 18-4-202 to 18-4-204; or

(c) The other person is committing or reasonably appears about to commit kidnapping as defined in section 18-3-301 or 18-3-302, robbery as defined in section 18-4-301 or 18-4-302, sexual assault as set forth in section 18-3-402, or in section 18-3-403 as it existed prior to July 1, 2000, or assault as defined in sections 18-3-202 and 18-3-203.

(3) Notwithstanding the provisions of subsection (1) of this section, a person is not justified in using physical force if:

(a) With intent to cause bodily injury or death to another person, he provokes the use of unlawful physical force by that other person; or

(b) He is the initial aggressor; except that his use of physical force upon another person under the circumstances is justifiable if he withdraws from the encounter and effectively communicates to the other person his intent to do so, but the latter nevertheless continues or threatens the use of unlawful physical force; or

(c) The physical force involved is the product of a combat by agreement not specifically authorized by law.

(4) In a case in which the defendant is not entitled to a jury instruction regarding self-defense as an affirmative defense, the court shall allow the defendant to present evidence, when relevant, that he or she was acting in self-defense. If the defendant presents evidence of self-defense, the court shall instruct the jury with a self-defense law instruction. The court shall instruct the jury that it may consider the evidence of self-defense in determining whether the defendant acted recklessly, with extreme indifference, or in a criminally negligent manner. However, the self-defense law instruction shall not be an affirmative defense instruction and the prosecuting attorney shall not have the burden of disproving self-defense. This section shall not apply to strict liability crimes.

Cross references: For limitations on civil suits against persons using physical force in defense of a person or to prevent the commission of a felony, see § 13-80-119.

18-1-704.5. Use of deadly physical force against an intruder.

(1) The general assembly hereby recognizes that the citizens of Colorado have a right to expect absolute safety within their own homes.

(2) Notwithstanding the provisions of section 18-1-704, any occupant of a dwelling is justified in using any degree of physical force, including deadly physical force, against another person when that other person has made an unlawful entry into the dwelling, and when the occupant has a reasonable belief that such other person has committed a crime in the dwelling in addition to the uninvited entry, or is committing or intends to commit a crime against a person or property in addition to the uninvited entry, and when the occupant reasonably believes that such other person might use any physical force, no matter how slight, against any occupant.

(3) Any occupant of a dwelling using physical force, including deadly physical force, in accordance with the provisions of subsection (2) of this section shall be immune from criminal prosecution for the use of such force.

(4) Any occupant of a dwelling using physical force, including deadly physical force, in accordance with the provisions of subsection (2) of this section shall be immune from any civil liability for injuries or death resulting from the use of such force.

18-1-705. Use of physical force in defense of premises.

A person in possession or control of any building, realty, or other premises, or a person who is licensed or privileged to be thereon, is justified in using reasonable and appropriate physical force upon another person when and to the extent that it is reasonably necessary to prevent or terminate what he reasonably believes to be the commission or attempted commission of an unlawful trespass by the other person in or upon the building, realty, or premises. However, he may use deadly force only in defense of himself or another as described in section 18-1-704, or when he reasonably believes it necessary to prevent what he reasonably believes to be an attempt by the trespasser to commit first degree arson.

18-1-706. Use of physical force in defense of property.

A person is justified in using reasonable and appropriate physical force upon another person when and to the extent that he reasonably believes it necessary to prevent what he reasonably believes to be an attempt by the other person to commit theft, criminal mischief, or criminal tampering involving property, but he may use deadly physical force under these circumstances only in defense of himself or another as described in section 18-1-704.

18-3-102. Murder in the first degree

(1) A person commits the crime of murder in the first degree if:

(a) After deliberation and with the intent to cause the death of a person other than himself, he causes the death of that person or of another person; or

(b) Acting either alone or with one or more persons, he or she commits or attempts to commit arson, robbery, burglary, kidnapping, sexual assault as prohibited by section 18-3-402, sexual assault in the first or second degree as prohibited by section 18-3-402 or 18-3-403 as those sections existed prior to July 1, 2000, or a class 3 felony for sexual assault on a child as provided in section 18-3-405 (2), or the crime of escape as provided in section 18-8-208, and, in the course of or in furtherance of the crime that he or she is committing or attempting to commit, or of immediate flight therefrom, the death of a person, other than one of the participants, is caused by anyone; or

(c) By perjury or subornation of perjury he procures the conviction and execution of any innocent person; or

(d) Under circumstances evidencing an attitude of universal malice manifesting extreme indifference to the value of human life generally, he knowingly engages in conduct which creates a grave risk of death to a person, or persons, other than himself, and thereby causes the death of another; or

(e) He or she commits unlawful distribution, dispensation, or sale of a controlled substance to a person under the age of eighteen years on school grounds as provided in section 18-18-407 (2), and the death of such person is caused by the use of such controlled substance; or

(f) The person knowingly causes the death of a child who has not yet attained twelve years of age and the person committing the offense is one in a position of trust with respect to the victim.

(2) It is an affirmative defense to a charge of violating subsection (1) (b) of this section that the defendant:

(a) Was not the only participant in the underlying crime; and

(b) Did not commit the homicidal act or in any way solicit, request, command, importune, cause, or aid the commission thereof; and

(c) Was not armed with a deadly weapon; and

(d) Had no reasonable ground to believe that any other participant was armed with such a weapon, instrument, article, or substance; and

(e) Did not engage himself in or intend to engage in and had no reasonable ground to believe that any other participant intended to engage in conduct likely to result in death or serious bodily injury; and

(f) Endeavored to disengage himself from the commission of the underlying crime or flight therefrom immediately upon having reasonable grounds to believe that another participant is armed with a deadly weapon, instrument, article, or substance, or intended to engage in conduct likely to result in death or serious bodily injury.

(3) Murder in the first degree is a class 1 felony.

(4) The statutory privilege between patient and physician and between husband and wife shall not be available for excluding or refusing testimony in any prosecution for the crime of murder in the first degree as described in paragraph (f) of subsection (1) of this section.

18-3-103. Murder in the second degree

(1) A person commits the crime of murder in the second degree if the person knowingly causes the death of a person.

(2) Diminished responsibility due to self-induced intoxication is not a defense to murder in the second degree.

(2.5) (Deleted by amendment, L. 96, p. 1844, § 12, effective July 1, 1996.)

(3) (a) Except as otherwise provided in paragraph (b) of this subsection (3), murder in the second degree is a class 2 felony.

(b) Notwithstanding the provisions of paragraph (a) of this subsection (3), murder in the second degree is a class 3 felony where the act causing the death was performed upon a sudden heat of passion, caused by a serious and highly provoking act of the intended victim, affecting the defendant sufficiently to excite an irresistible passion in a reasonable person; but, if between the provocation and the killing there is an interval sufficient for the voice of reason and humanity to be heard, the killing is a class 2 felony.

(4) A defendant convicted pursuant to subsection (1) of this section shall be sentenced by the court in accordance with the provisions of section 18-1.3-406.

18-3-104. Manslaughter

(1) A person commits the crime of manslaughter if:

(a) Such person recklessly causes the death of another person; or

(b) Such person intentionally causes or aids another person to commit suicide.

(c) (Deleted by amendment, L. 96, p. 1844, § 13, effective July 1, 1996.)

(2) Manslaughter is a class 4 felony.

(3) This section shall not apply to a person, including a proxy decision-maker as such person is described in section 15-18.5-103, C.R.S., who complies with any advance medical directive in accordance with the provisions of title 15, C.R.S., including a medical durable power of attorney, a living will, or a cardiopulmonary resuscitation (CPR) directive.

(4) (a) This section shall not apply to a medical caregiver with prescriptive authority or authority to administer medication who prescribes or administers medication for palliative care to a terminally ill patient with the consent of the terminally ill patient or his or her agent.

(b) For purposes of this subsection (4):

(I) "Agent" means a person appointed to represent the interests of the terminally ill patient by a medical power of attorney, power of attorney, health care proxy, or any other similar statutory or regular procedure used for designation of such person.

(II) "Medical caregiver" means a physician, registered nurse, nurse practitioner, physician assistant, or anesthesiologist assistant licensed by this state.

(III) "Palliative care" means medical care and treatment provided by a licensed medical caregiver to a patient with an advanced chronic or terminal illness whose condition may not be responsive to curative treatment and who is, therefore, receiving treatment that relieves pain and suffering and supports the best possible quality of his or her life.

(c) Paragraph (a) of this subsection (4) shall not be interpreted to permit a medical caregiver to assist in the suicide of the patient.

18-3-105. Criminally negligent homicide

Any person who causes the death of another person by conduct amounting to criminal negligence commits criminally negligent homicide which is a class 5 felony.

18-3-206. Menacing

(1) A person commits the crime of menacing if, by any threat of physical action, he or she knowingly places of attempts to place another person in fear of imminent serious bodily injury. Menacing is a class 3 misdemeanor, but, it is a class 5 felony if committed:

(a) By the use of a deadly weapon or any article used or fashioned in a manner to cause a person to reasonably believe that article is a deadly weapon; or

(b) By the person representing verbally or otherwise that he or she is armed with a deadly weapon

18-3-208. Reckless endangerment.

A person who recklessly engages in conduct which creates a substantial risk of serious bodily injury to another person commits reckless endangerment, which is a class 3 misdemeanor.

18-3-301. First degree kidnapping.

(1) Any person who does any of the following acts with the intent thereby to force the victim or any other person to make any concession or give up anything of value in order to secure a release of a person under the offender's actual or apparent control commits first degree kidnapping:

(a) Forcibly seizes and carries any person from one place to another; or

(b) Entices or persuades any person to go from one place to another; or

(c) Imprisons or forcibly secretes any person.

(2) Whoever commits first degree kidnapping is guilty of a class 1 felony if the person kidnapped shall have suffered bodily injury; but no person convicted of first degree kidnapping shall suffer the death penalty if the person kidnapped was liberated alive prior to the conviction of the kidnapper.

(3) Whoever commits first degree kidnapping commits a class 2 felony if, prior to his conviction, the person kidnapped was liberated unharmed.

18-3-303. False imprisonment.

(1) Any person who knowingly confines or detains another without the other's consent and without proper legal authority commits false imprisonment. This section shall not apply to a peace officer acting in good faith within the scope of his or her duties.

(2) False imprisonment is a class 2 misdemeanor; except that false imprisonment is a class 5 felony if:

(a) The person uses force or threat of force to confine or detain the other person; and

(b) The person confines or detains the other person for twelve hours or longer.

18-4-101. Definitions.

As used in this article, unless the context otherwise requires:

(1) "Building" means a structure which has the capacity to contain, and is designed for the shelter of, man, animals, or property, and includes a ship, trailer, sleeping car, airplane, or other vehicle or place adapted for overnight accommodations of persons or animals, or for carrying on of business therein, whether or not a person or animal is actually present.

(2) "Occupied structure" means any area, place, facility, or enclosure which, for particular purposes, may be used by persons or animals upon occasion, whether or not included within the definition of "building" in subsection (1) of this section, and which is in fact occupied by a person or animal, and known by the defendant to be thus occupied at the time he acts in violation of one or more of sections 18-4-102 to 18-4-105.

(3) Property is that of "another" if anyone other than the defendant has a possessory or proprietary interest therein.

(4) If a building is divided into units for separate occupancy, any unit not occupied by the defendant is a "building of another".

18-4-102. First degree arson.

(1) A person who knowingly sets fire to, burns, causes to be burned, or by the use of any explosive damages or destroys, or causes to be damaged or destroyed, any building or occupied structure of another without his consent commits first degree arson.

(2) First degree arson is a class 3 felony.

(3) A defendant convicted of committing first degree arson by the use of any explosive shall be sentenced

18-4-201. Definitions.

As used in this article, unless the context otherwise requires:

(1) "Premises" means any real estate and all improvements erected thereon.

(2) "Separate building" means each unit of a building consisting of two or more units separately secured or occupied.

(3) A person "enters unlawfully" or "remains unlawfully" in or upon premises when the person is not licensed, invited, or otherwise privileged to do so. A person who, regardless of his or her intent, enters or remains in or upon premises that are at the time open to the public does so with license and privilege unless the person defies a lawful order not to enter or remain, personally communicated to him or her by the owner of the premises or some other authorized person. A license or privilege to enter or remain in a building that is only partly open to the public is not a license or privilege to enter or remain in that part of the building that is not open to the public. Except as is otherwise provided in section 33-6-116 (1), C.R.S., a person who enters or remains upon unimproved and apparently unused land that is neither fenced nor otherwise enclosed in a manner designed to exclude intruders does so with license and privilege unless notice against trespass is personally communicated to the person by the owner of the land or some other authorized person or unless notice forbidding entry is given by posting with signs at intervals of not more than four hundred forty yards or, if there is a readily identifiable entrance to the land, by posting with signs at such entrance to the private land or the forbidden part of the land. In the case of a designated access road not otherwise posted, said notice shall be posted at the entrance to private land and shall be substantially as follows:

"ENTERING PRIVATE PROPERTY REMAIN ON ROADS".

18-12-101. Definitions.

(1) As used in this article, unless the context otherwise requires:

(a) "Adult" means any person eighteen years of age or older.

(a.3) "Ballistic knife" means any knife that has a blade which is forcefully projected from the handle by means of a spring-loaded device or explosive charge.

(a.5) "Blackjack" includes any billy, sand club, sandbag, or other hand-operated striking weapon consisting, at the striking end, of an encased piece of lead or other heavy substance and, at the handle end, a strap or springy shaft which increases the force of impact.

(b) "Bomb" means any explosive or incendiary device or molotov cocktail as defined in section 9-7-103, C.R.S., or any chemical device which causes or can cause an explosion, which is not specifically designed for lawful and legitimate use in the hands of its possessor.

(c) "Firearm silencer" means any instrument, attachment, weapon, or appliance for causing the firing of any gun, revolver, pistol, or other firearm to be silent or intended to lessen or muffle the noise of the firing of any such weapon.

(d) "Gas gun" means a device designed for projecting gas-filled projectiles which release their contents after having been projected from the device and includes projectiles designed for use in such a device.

(e) "Gravity knife" means any knife that has a blade released from the handle or sheath thereof by the force of gravity or the application of centrifugal force, that when released is locked in place by means of a button, spring, lever, or other device.

(e.5) "Handgun" means a pistol, revolver, or other firearm of any description, loaded or unloaded, from which any shot, bullet, or other missile can be discharged, the length of the barrel of which, not including any revolving, detachable, or magazine breech, does not exceed twelve inches.

(e.7) "Juvenile" means any person under the age of eighteen years.

(f) "Knife" means any dagger, dirk, knife, or stiletto with a blade over three and one-half inches in length, or any other dangerous instrument capable of inflicting cutting, stabbing, or tearing wounds, but does not include a hunting or fishing knife carried for sports use. The issue that a knife is a hunting or fishing knife must be raised as an affirmative defense.

(g) "Machine gun" means any firearm, whatever its size and usual designation, that shoots automatically more than one shot, without manual reloading, by a single function of the trigger.

(h) "Short rifle" means a rifle having a barrel less than sixteen inches long or an overall length of less than twenty-six inches.

(i) "Short shotgun" means a shotgun having a barrel or barrels less than eighteen inches long or an overall length of less than twenty-six inches.

(i.5) "Stun gun" means a device capable of temporarily immobilizing a person by the infliction of an electrical charge.

(j) "Switchblade knife" means any knife, the blade of which opens automatically by hand pressure applied to a button, spring, or other device in its handle.

(2) It shall be an affirmative defense to any provision of this article that the act was committed by a peace officer in the lawful discharge of his duties.

18-12-105. Unlawfully carrying a concealed weapon - unlawful possession of weapons.

(1) A person commits a class 2 misdemeanor if such person knowingly and unlawfully:

(a) Carries a knife concealed on or about his or her person; or

(b) Carries a firearm concealed on or about his or her person; or

(c) Without legal authority, carries, brings, or has in such person's possession a firearm or any explosive, incendiary, or other dangerous device on the property of or within any building in which the chambers, galleries, or offices of the general assembly, or either house thereof, are located, or in which a legislative hearing or meeting is being or is to be conducted, or in which the official office of any member, officer, or employee of the general assembly is located.

(d) (Deleted by amendment, L. 93, p. 964, § 1, effective July 1, 1993.)

(2) It shall not be an offense if the defendant was:

(a) A person in his or her own dwelling or place of business or on property owned or under his or her control at the time of the act of carrying; or

(b) A person in a private automobile or other private means of conveyance who carries a weapon for lawful protection of such person's or another's person or property while traveling; or

(c) A person who, at the time of carrying a concealed weapon, held a valid written permit to carry a concealed weapon issued pursuant to section 18-12-105.1, as it existed prior to its repeal, or, if the weapon involved was a handgun, held a valid permit to carry a concealed handgun or a temporary emergency permit issued pursuant to part 2 of this article; except that it shall be an offense under this section if the person was carrying a concealed handgun in violation of the provisions of section 18-12-214; or

(d) A peace officer, as described in section 16-2.5-101, C.R.S., when carrying a weapon in conformance with the policy of the employing agency as provided in section 16-2.5-101 (2), C.R.S.; or

(e) (Deleted by amendment, L. 2003, p. 1624, § 46, effective August 6, 2003.)

(f) A United States probation officer or a United States pretrial services officer while on duty and serving in the state of Colorado under the authority of rules and regulations promulgated by the judicial conference of the United States.

18-12-105.5. Unlawfully carrying a weapon - unlawful possession of weapons - school, college, or university grounds.

(1) A person commits a class 6 felony if such person knowingly and unlawfully and without legal authority carries, brings, or has in such person's possession a deadly weapon as defined in section 18-1-901 (3) (e) in or on the real estate and all improvements erected thereon of any public or private elementary, middle, junior high, high, or vocational school or any public or private college, university, or seminary, except for the purpose of presenting an authorized public demonstration or exhibition pursuant to instruction in conjunction with an organized school or class, for the purpose of carrying out the necessary duties and functions of an employee of an educational institution that require the use of a deadly weapon, or for the purpose of participation in an authorized extracurricular activity or on an athletic team.

(2) (Deleted by amendment, L. 2000, p. 709, § 45, effective July 1, 2000.)

(3) It shall not be an offense under this section if:

(a) The weapon is unloaded and remains inside a motor vehicle while upon the real estate of any public or private college, university, or seminary; or

(b) The person is in that person's own dwelling or place of business or on property owned or under that person's control at the time of the act of carrying; or

(c) The person is in a private automobile or other private means of conveyance and is carrying a weapon for lawful protection of that person's or another's person or property while traveling; or

(d) The person, at the time of carrying a concealed weapon, held a valid written permit to carry a concealed weapon issued pursuant to section 18-12-105.1, as said section existed prior to its repeal; except that it shall be an offense under this section if the person was carrying a concealed handgun in violation of the provisions of section 18-12-214 (3); or

(d.5) The weapon involved was a handgun and the person held a valid permit to carry a concealed handgun or a temporary emergency permit issued pursuant to part 2 of this article; except that it shall be an offense under this section if the person was carrying a concealed handgun in violation of the provisions of section 18-12-214 (3); or

(e) The person is a peace officer, as described in section 16-2.5-101, C.R.S., when carrying a weapon in conformance with the policy of the employing agency as provided in section 16-2.5-101 (2), C.R.S.; or

(f) and (g) (Deleted by amendment, L. 2003, p. 1626, § 51, effective August 6, 2003.)

(h) The person has possession of the weapon for use in an educational program approved by a school which program includes, but shall not be limited to, any course designed for the repair or maintenance of weapons.

18-12-105.6. Limitation on local ordinances regarding firearms in private vehicles.

(1) The general assembly hereby finds that:

(a) A person carrying a weapon in a private automobile or other private means of conveyance for hunting or for lawful protection of such person's or another's person or property, as permitted in sections 18-12-105 (2) (b) and 18-12-105.5 (3) (c), may tend to travel within a county, city and county, or municipal jurisdiction or in or through different county, city and county, and municipal jurisdictions, en route to the person's destination;

(b) Inconsistent laws exist in local jurisdictions with regard to the circumstances under which weapons may be carried in automobiles and other private means of conveyance;

(c) This inconsistency creates a confusing patchwork of laws that unfairly subjects a person who lawfully travels with a weapon to criminal penalties because he or she travels within a jurisdiction or into or through another jurisdiction;

(d) This inconsistency places citizens in the position of not knowing when they may be violating local laws while traveling within a jurisdiction or in, through, or between different jurisdictions, and therefore being unable to avoid committing a crime.

(2) (a) Based on the findings specified in subsection (1) of this section, the general assembly concludes that the carrying of weapons in private automobiles or other private means of conveyance for hunting or for lawful protection of a person's or another's person or property while traveling into, through, or within, a municipal, county, or city and county jurisdiction, regardless of the number of times the person stops in a jurisdiction, is a matter of statewide concern and is not an offense.

(b) Notwithstanding any other provision of law, no municipality, county, or city and county shall have the authority to enact or enforce any ordinance or resolution that would restrict a person's ability to travel with a weapon in a private automobile or other private means of conveyance for hunting or for lawful protection of a person's or another's person or property while traveling into, through, or within, a municipal, county, or city and county jurisdiction, regardless of the number of times the person stops in a jurisdiction.

18-12-106. Prohibited use of weapons.

(1) A person commits a class 2 misdemeanor if:

(a) He knowingly and unlawfully aims a firearm at another person; or

(b) Recklessly or with criminal negligence he discharges a firearm or shoots a bow and arrow; or

(c) He knowingly sets a loaded gun, trap, or device designed to cause an explosion upon being tripped or approached, and leaves it unattended by a competent person immediately present; or

(d) The person has in his or her possession a firearm while the person is under the influence of intoxicating liquor or of a controlled substance, as defined in section 12-22-303 (7), C.R.S. Possession of a permit issued under section 18-12-105.1, as it existed prior to its repeal, or possession of a permit or a temporary emergency permit issued pursuant to part 2 of this article is no defense to a violation of this subsection (1).

(e) He knowingly aims, swings, or throws a throwing star or nunchaku as defined in this paragraph (e) at another person, or he knowingly possesses a throwing star or nunchaku in a public place except for the purpose of presenting an authorized public demonstration or exhibition or pursuant to instruction in conjunction with an organized school or class. When transporting throwing stars or nunchaku for a public demonstration or exhibition or for a school or class, they shall be transported in a closed, nonaccessible container. For purposes of this paragraph (e), "nunchaku" means an instrument consisting of two sticks, clubs, bars, or rods to be used as handles, connected by a rope, cord, wire, or chain, which is in the design of a weapon used in connection with the practice of a system of self-defense, and "throwing star" means a disk having sharp radiating points or any disk-shaped bladed object which is hand-held and thrown and which is in the design of a weapon used in connection with the practice of a system of self-defense.

18-12-108.7. Unlawfully providing or permitting a juvenile to possess a handgun - penalty - unlawfully providing a firearm other than a handgun to a juvenile - penalty.

(1) (a) Any person who intentionally, knowingly, or recklessly provides a handgun with or without remuneration to any person under the age of eighteen years in violation of section 18-12-108.5 or any person who knows of such juvenile's conduct which violates section 18-12-108.5 and fails to make reasonable efforts to pre-

vent such violation commits the crime of unlawfully providing a handgun to a juvenile or permitting a juvenile to possess a handgun.

(b) Unlawfully providing a handgun to a juvenile or permitting a juvenile to possess a handgun in violation of this subsection (1) is a class 4 felony.

(2) (a) Any person who intentionally, knowingly, or recklessly provides a handgun to a juvenile or permits a juvenile to possess a handgun, even though such person is aware of a substantial risk that such juvenile will use a handgun to commit a felony offense, or who, being aware of such substantial risk, fails to make reasonable efforts to prevent the commission of the offense, commits the crime of unlawfully providing or permitting a juvenile to possess a handgun. A person shall be deemed to have violated this paragraph (a) if such person provides a handgun to or permits the possession of a handgun by any juvenile who has been convicted of a crime of violence, as defined in section 18-1.3-406, or any juvenile who has been adjudicated a juvenile delinquent for an offense which would constitute a crime of violence, as defined in section 18-1.3-406, if such juvenile were an adult.

(b) Unlawfully providing a handgun to a juvenile or permitting a juvenile to possess a handgun in violation of this subsection (2) is a class 4 felony.

(3) With regard to firearms other than handguns, no person shall sell, rent, or transfer ownership or allow unsupervised possession of a firearm with or without remuneration to any juvenile without the consent of the juvenile's parent or legal guardian. Unlawfully providing a firearm other than a handgun to a juvenile in violation of this subsection (3) is a class 1 misdemeanor.

(4) It shall not be an offense under this section if a person believes that a juvenile will physically harm the person if the person attempts to disarm the juvenile or prevent the juvenile from committing a violation of section 18-12-108.5.

18-12-112. Private firearms transfers - background check required - penalty – definitions

(1) (a) On and after July 1, 2013, except as described in subsection (6) of this section, before any person who is not a licensed gun dealer, as defined in section 12-26.1-106 (6), C.R.S., transfers or attempts to transfer possession of a firearm to a transferee, he or she shall:

(I) Require that a background check, in accordance with section 24-33.5-424, C.R.S., be conducted of the prospective transferee; and

(II) Obtain approval of a transfer from the bureau after a background check has been requested by a licensed gun dealer, in accordance with section 24-33.5-424, C.R.S.

(b) As used in this section, unless the context requires otherwise, "transferee" means a person who desires to receive or acquire a firearm from a transferor. If a transferee is not a natural person, then each natural person who is authorized by the transferee to possess the firearm after the transfer shall undergo a background check, as described in paragraph (a) of this subsection (1), before taking possession of the firearm.

(2) (a) A prospective firearm transferor who is not a licensed gun dealer shall arrange for a licensed gun dealer to obtain the background check required by this section.

(b) A licensed gun dealer who obtains a background check on a prospective transferee shall record the transfer, as provided in section 12-26-102, C.R.S., and retain the records, as provided in section 12-26-103, C.R.S., in the same manner as when conducting a sale, rental, or exchange at retail. The licensed gun dealer shall comply with all state and federal laws, including 18 U.S.C. sec. 922, as if he or she were transferring the firearm from his or her inventory to the prospective transferee.

(c) A licensed gun dealer who obtains a background check for a prospective firearm transferor pursuant to this section shall provide the firearm transferor and transferee a copy of the results of the background check, including the bureau's approval or disapproval of the transfer.

(d) A licensed gun dealer may charge a fee for services rendered pursuant to this section, which fee shall not exceed ten dollars.

(3) (a) A prospective firearm transferee under this section shall not accept possession of the firearm unless the prospective firearm transferor has obtained approval of the transfer from the bureau after a background check has been requested by a licensed gun dealer, as described in paragraph (b) of subsection (1) of this section.

(b) A prospective firearm transferee shall not knowingly provide false information to a prospective firearm transferor or to a licensed gun dealer for the purpose of acquiring a firearm.

(4) If the bureau approves a transfer of a firearm pursuant to this section, the approval shall be valid for thirty calendar days, during which time the transferor and transferee may complete the transfer.

(5) A person who transfers a firearm in violation of the provisions of this section may be jointly and severally liable for any civil damages proximately caused by the transferee's subsequent use of the firearm.

(6) The provisions of this section do not apply to:

(a) A transfer of an antique firearm, as defined in 18 U.S.C. sec. 921(a) (16), as amended, or a curio or relic, as defined in 27 CFR 478.11, as amended;

(b) A transfer that is a bona fide gift or loan between immediate family members, which are limited to spouses, parents, children, siblings, grandparents, grandchildren, nieces, nephews, first cousins, aunts, and uncles;

(c) A transfer that occurs by operation of law or because of the death of a person for whom the prospective transferor is an executor or administrator of an estate or a trustee of a trust created in a will;

(d) A transfer that is temporary and occurs while in the home of the unlicensed transferee if:

(I) The unlicensed transferee is not prohibited from possessing firearms; and

(II) The unlicensed transferee reasonably believes that possession of the firearm is necessary to prevent imminent death or serious bodily injury to the unlicensed transferee;

(e) A temporary transfer of possession without transfer of ownership or a title to ownership, which transfer takes place:

(I) At a shooting range located in or on premises owned or occupied by a duly incorporated organization organized for conservation purposes or to foster proficiency in firearms;

(II) At a target firearm shooting competition under the auspices of, or approved by, a state agency or a nonprofit organization; or

(III) While hunting, fishing, target shooting, or trapping if:

(A) The hunting, fishing, target shooting, or trapping is legal in all places where the unlicensed transferee possesses the firearm; and

(B) The unlicensed transferee holds any license or permit that is required for such hunting, fishing, target shooting, or trapping;

(f) A transfer of a firearm that is made to facilitate the repair or maintenance of the firearm; except that this paragraph (f) does not apply unless all parties who possess the firearm as a result of the transfer may legally possess a firearm;

(g) Any temporary transfer that occurs while in the continuous presence of the owner of the firearm;

(h) A temporary transfer for not more than seventy-two hours. A person who transfers a firearm pursuant to this paragraph (h) may be jointly and severally liable for damages proximately caused by the transferee's subsequent unlawful use of the firearm; or

(i) A transfer of a firearm from a person serving in the armed forces of the United States who will be deployed outside of the United States within the next thirty days to any immediate family member, which is limited to a spouse, parent, child, sibling, grandparent, grandchild, niece, nephew, first cousin, aunt, and uncle of the person.

(7) For purposes of paragraph (f) of subsection (6) of this section:

(a) An owner, manager, or employee of a business that repairs or maintains firearms may rely upon a transferor's statement that he or she may legally possess a firearm unless the owner, manager, or employee has actual knowledge to the contrary and may return possession of the firearm to the transferor upon completion of the repairs or maintenance without a background check;

(b) Unless a transferor of a firearm has actual knowledge to the contrary, the transferor may rely upon the statement of an owner, manager, or employee of a business that repairs or maintains firearms that no owner, manager, or employee of the business is prohibited from possessing a firearm.

(8) Nothing in subsection (6) of this section shall be interpreted to limit or otherwise alter the applicability of section 18-12-111 concerning the unlawful purchase or transfer of firearms.

(9) (a) A person who violates a provision of this section commits a class 1 misdemeanor and shall be punished in accordance with section 18-1.3-501. The person shall also be prohibited from possessing a firearm for two years, beginning on the date of his or her conviction.

(b) When a person is convicted of violating a provision of this section, the state court administrator shall report the conviction to the bureau and to the national instant criminal background check system created by the federal "Brady Handgun Violence Prevention Act", Pub.L. 103-159, the relevant portion of which is codified at 18 U.S.C. sec. 922 (t). The report shall include information indicating that the person is prohibited from possessing a firearm for two years, beginning on the date of his or her conviction.

18-12-202. Definitions.

As used in this part 2, unless the context otherwise requires:

(1) Repealed.

(2) "Certified instructor" means an instructor for a firearms safety course who is certified as a firearms instructor by:

(a) A county, municipal, state, or federal law enforcement agency;

(b) The peace officers standards and training board created in section 24-31-302, C.R.S.;

(c) A federal military agency; or

(d) A national nonprofit organization that certifies firearms instructors, operates national firearms competitions, and provides training, including courses in personal protection, in small arms safety, use, and marksmanship.

(3) "Chronically and habitually uses alcoholic beverages to the extent that the applicant's normal faculties are impaired" means:

(a) The applicant has at any time been committed as an alcoholic pursuant to section 27-81-111 or 27-81-112, C.R.S.; or

(b) Within the ten-year period immediately preceding the date on which the permit application is submitted, the applicant:

(I) Has been committed as an alcoholic pursuant to section 27-81-109 or 27-81-110, C.R.S.; or

(II) Has had two or more alcohol-related convictions under section 42-4-1301 (1) or (2), C.R.S., or a law of another state that has similar elements, or revocations related to misdemeanor, alcohol-related convictions under section 42-2-126, C.R.S., or a law of another state that has similar elements.

(4) "Handgun" means a handgun as defined in section 18-12-101 (1) (e.5); except that the term does not include a machine gun as defined in section 18-12-101 (1) (g).

(5) (a) "Handgun training class" means:

(I) A law enforcement training firearms safety course;

(II) A firearms safety course offered by a law enforcement agency, an institution of higher education, or a public or private institution or organization or firearms training school, that is open to the general public and is taught by a certified instructor; or

(III) A firearms safety course or class that is offered and taught by a certified instructor.

(b) Notwithstanding paragraph (a) of this subsection (5), "handgun training class" does not include any firearms safety course that allows a person to complete the entire course:

(I) Via the internet or an electronic device; or

(II) In any location other than the physical location where the certified instructor offers the course.

(6) "Permit" means a permit to carry a concealed handgun issued pursuant to the provisions of this part 2; except that "permit" does not include a temporary emergency permit issued pursuant to section 18-12-209.

(7) "Sheriff" means the sheriff of a county, or his or her designee, or the official who has the duties of a sheriff in a city and county, or his or her designee.

(8) "Training certificate" means a certificate, affidavit, or other document issued by the instructor, school, club, or organization that conducts a handgun training class that evidences an applicant's successful completion of the class requirements.

18-12-203. Criteria for obtaining a permit.

(1) Beginning May 17, 2003, except as otherwise provided in this section, a sheriff shall issue a permit to carry a concealed handgun to an applicant who:

(a) Is a legal resident of the state of Colorado. For purposes of this part 2, a person who is a member of the armed forces and is stationed pursuant to permanent duty station orders at a military installation in this state, and a member of the person's immediate family living in Colorado, shall be deemed to be a legal resident of the state of Colorado.

(b) Is twenty-one years of age or older;

(c) Is not ineligible to possess a firearm pursuant to section 18-12-108 or federal law;

(d) Has not been convicted of perjury under section 18-8-503, in relation to information provided or deliberately omitted on a permit application submitted pursuant to this part 2;

(e) (I) Does not chronically and habitually use alcoholic beverages to the extent that the applicant's normal faculties are impaired.

(II) The prohibition specified in this paragraph (e) shall not apply to an applicant who provides an affidavit, signed by a professional counselor who is licensed pursuant to article 43 of title 12, C.R.S., and specializes in alcohol addiction, stating that the applicant has been evaluated by the counselor and has been determined to be a recovering alcoholic who has refrained from using alcohol for at least three years.

(f) Is not an unlawful user of or addicted to a controlled substance as defined in section 18-18-102 (5). Whether an applicant is an unlawful user of or addicted to a controlled substance shall be determined as provided in federal law and regulations.

(g) Is not subject to:

(I) A protection order issued pursuant to section 18-1-1001 or section 19-2-707, C.R.S., that is in effect at the time the application is submitted; or

(II) A permanent protection order issued pursuant to article 14 of title 13, C.R.S.; or

(III) A temporary protection order issued pursuant to article 14 of title 13, C.R.S., that is in effect at the time the application is submitted;

(h) Demonstrates competence with a handgun by submitting:

(I) Evidence of experience with a firearm through participation in organized shooting competitions or current military service;

(II) Evidence that, at the time the application is submitted, the applicant is a certified instructor;

(III) Proof of honorable discharge from a branch of the United States armed forces within the three years preceding submittal of the application;

(IV) Proof of honorable discharge from a branch of the United States armed forces that reflects pistol qualifications obtained within the ten years preceding submittal of the application;

(V) A certificate showing retirement from a Colorado law enforcement agency that reflects pistol qualifications obtained within the ten years preceding submittal of the application; or

(VI) A training certificate from a handgun training class obtained within the ten years preceding submittal of the application. The applicant shall submit the original training certificate or a photocopy thereof that includes the original signature of the class instructor. In obtaining a training certificate from a handgun training class, the applicant shall have discretion in selecting which handgun training class to complete.

(2) Regardless of whether an applicant meets the criteria specified in subsection (1) of this section, if the sheriff has a reasonable belief that documented previous behavior by the applicant makes it likely the applicant will present a danger to self or others if the

applicant receives a permit to carry a concealed handgun, the sheriff may deny the permit.

(3) (a) The sheriff shall deny, revoke, or refuse to renew a permit if an applicant or a permittee fails to meet one of the criteria listed in subsection (1) of this section and may deny, revoke, or refuse to renew a permit on the grounds specified in subsection (2) of this section.

(b) Following issuance of a permit, if the issuing sheriff has a reasonable belief that a permittee no longer meets the criteria specified in subsection (1) of this section or that the permittee presents a danger as described in subsection (2) of this section, the sheriff shall suspend the permit until such time as the matter is resolved and the issuing sheriff determines that the permittee is eligible to possess a permit as provided in this section.

(c) If the sheriff suspends or revokes a permit, the sheriff shall notify the permittee in writing, stating the grounds for suspension or revocation and informing the permittee of the right to seek a second review by the sheriff, to submit additional information for the record, and to seek judicial review pursuant to section 18-12-207.

18-12-207. Judicial review - permit denial - permit suspension - permit revocation.

(1) If a sheriff denies a permit application, refuses to renew a permit, or suspends or revokes a permit, the applicant or permittee may seek judicial review of the sheriff's decision. The applicant or permittee may seek judicial review either in lieu of or subsequent to the sheriff's second review.

(2) The procedure and time lines for filing a complaint, an answer, and briefs for judicial review pursuant to this section shall be in accordance with the procedures specified in rule 106 (a) (4) and (b) of the Colorado rules of civil procedure.

(3) Notwithstanding any other provision of law to the contrary, at a judicial review sought pursuant to this section, the sheriff shall have the burden of proving by a preponderance of the evidence that the applicant or permittee is ineligible to possess a permit under the criteria listed in section 18-12-203 (1) or, if the denial, sus-

pension, or revocation was based on the sheriff's determination that the person would be a danger as provided in section 18-12-203 (2), the sheriff shall have the burden of proving the determination by clear and convincing evidence. Following completion of the review, the court may award attorney fees to the prevailing party.

18-12-211. Renewal of permits.

(1) Within one hundred twenty days prior to expiration of a permit, the permittee may obtain a renewal form from the issuing sheriff and renew the permit by submitting to the issuing sheriff a completed renewal form, a notarized affidavit stating that the permittee remains qualified pursuant to the criteria specified in section 18-12-203 (1) (a) to (1) (g), and the required renewal fee not to exceed fifty dollars, as set by the sheriff pursuant to section 18-12-205 (5). The renewal form shall meet the requirements specified in section 18-12-205 (1) for an application. The sheriff shall verify pursuant to section 18-12-205 (4) that the permittee meets the criteria specified in section 18-12-203 (1) (a) to (1) (g) and is not a danger as described in section 18-12-203 (2) and shall either renew or deny the renewal of the permit in accordance with the provisions of section 18-12-206 (1). If the sheriff denies renewal of a permit, the permittee may seek a second review of the renewal application by the sheriff and may submit additional information for the record. The permittee may also seek judicial review as provided in section 18-12-207.

(2) A permittee who fails to file a renewal form on or before the permit expiration date may renew the permit by paying a late fee of fifteen dollars in addition to the renewal fee established pursuant to subsection (1) of this section. No permit shall be renewed six months or more after its expiration date, and the permit shall be deemed to have permanently expired. A person whose permit has permanently expired may reapply for a permit, but the person shall submit an application for a permit and the fee required pursuant to section 18-12-205. A person who knowingly and intentionally files false or misleading information or deliberately omits material information required under this section is subject to criminal prosecution for perjury under section 18-8-503.

18-12-213. Reciprocity.

A permit to carry a concealed handgun or a concealed weapon that is issued to a person twenty-one years of age or older by a state that recognizes the validity of permits issued pursuant to this part 2 shall be valid in this state in all respects as a permit issued pursuant to this part 2.

18-12-214. Authority granted by permit - carrying restrictions.

(1) (a) A permit to carry a concealed handgun authorizes the permittee to carry a concealed handgun in all areas of the state, except as specifically limited in this section. A permit does not authorize the permittee to use a handgun in a manner that would violate a provision of state law. A local government does not have authority to adopt or enforce an ordinance or resolution that would conflict with any provision of this part 2.

(b) A peace officer may temporarily disarm a permittee, incident to a lawful stop of the permittee. The peace officer shall return the handgun to the permittee prior to discharging the permittee from the scene.

(2) A permit issued pursuant to this part 2 does not authorize a person to carry a concealed handgun into a place where the carrying of firearms is prohibited by federal law.

(3) A permit issued pursuant to this part 2 does not authorize a person to carry a concealed handgun onto the real property, or into any improvements erected thereon, of a public elementary, middle, junior high, or high school; except that:

(a) A permittee may have a handgun on the real property of the public school so long as the handgun remains in his or her vehicle and, if the permittee is not in the vehicle, the handgun is in a compartment within the vehicle and the vehicle is locked.

(b) A permittee who is employed or retained by contract by a school district as a school security officer may carry a concealed handgun onto the real property, or into any improvement erected thereon, of a public elementary, middle, junior high, or high school while the permittee is on duty.

(c) A permittee may carry a concealed handgun on undeveloped real property owned by a school district that is used for hunting or other shooting sports.

(4) A permit issued pursuant to this part 2 does not authorize a person to carry a concealed handgun into a public building at which:

(a) Security personnel and electronic weapons screening devices are permanently in place at each entrance to the building;

(b) Security personnel electronically screen each person who enters the building to determine whether the person is carrying a weapon of any kind; and

(c) Security personnel require each person who is carrying a weapon of any kind to leave the weapon in possession of security personnel while the person is in the building.

(5) Nothing in this part 2 shall be construed to limit, restrict, or prohibit in any manner the existing rights of a private property owner, private tenant, private employer, or private business entity.

(6) The provisions of this section apply to temporary emergency permits issued pursuant to section 18-12-209.

18-12-216. Permits issued prior to May 17, 2003.

(1) A permit issued pursuant to section 18-12-105.1, as it existed prior to its repeal, shall permanently expire on June 30, 2007, or on the expiration date specified on the permit, whichever occurs first. A person who submitted a full set of fingerprints to obtain a permit prior to May 17, 2003, upon expiration of the permit, may apply for renewal of the permit as provided in this part 2. A person who did not submit a full set of fingerprints to obtain a permit prior to May 17, 2003, upon expiration of the permit, may apply for a new permit as provided in this part 2.

(2) Within one hundred twenty days prior to the expiration of a permit issued pursuant to section 18-12-105.1, as it existed prior to its repeal, the issuing authority shall send a notice of expiration to the permittee to notify the permittee of the permit expiration as provided in subsection (1) of this section and of his or her ability to renew the permit or obtain a new permit as provided in subsection (1) of this section.

18-12-301. Definitions

As used in this part 3, unless the context otherwise requires:

(1) "Bureau" means the Colorado bureau of investigation created and existing pursuant to section 24-33.5-401, C.R.S.

(2) (a) "Large-capacity magazine" means:

(I) A fixed or detachable magazine, box, drum, feed strip, or similar device capable of accepting, or that is designed to be readily converted to accept, more than fifteen rounds of ammunition;

(II) A fixed, tubular shotgun magazine that holds more than twenty-eight inches of shotgun shells, including any extension device that is attached to the magazine and holds additional shotgun shells; or

(III) A nontubular, detachable magazine, box, drum, feed strip, or similar device that is capable of accepting more than eight shotgun shells when combined with a fixed magazine.

(b) "Large-capacity magazine" does not mean:

(I) A feeding device that has been permanently altered so that it cannot accommodate more than fifteen rounds of ammunition;

(II) An attached tubular device designed to accept, and capable of operating only with, .22 caliber rimfire ammunition; or

(III) A tubular magazine that is contained in a lever-action firearm.

18-12-302. Large-capacity magazines prohibited - penalties – exceptions

(1) (a) Except as otherwise provided in this section, on and after July 1, 2013, a person who sells, transfers, or possesses a large-capacity magazine commits a class 2 misdemeanor.

(b) Any person who violates this subsection (1) after having been convicted of a prior violation of said subsection (1) commits a class 1 misdemeanor.

(c) Any person who violates this subsection (1) commits a class 6 felony if the person possessed a large-capacity magazine during the commission of a felony or any crime of violence, as defined in section 18-1.3-406.

(2) (a) A person may possess a large-capacity magazine if he or she:

(I) Owns the large-capacity magazine on July 1, 2013; and

(II) Maintains continuous possession of the large-capacity magazine.

(b) If a person who is alleged to have violated subsection (1) of this section asserts that he or she is permitted to legally possess a large-capacity magazine pursuant to paragraph (a) of this subsection (2), the prosecution has the burden of proof to refute the assertion.

(3) The offense described in subsection (1) of this section shall not apply to:

(a) An entity, or any employee thereof engaged in his or her employment duties, that manufactures large-capacity magazines within Colorado exclusively for transfer to, or any licensed gun dealer, as defined in section 12-26.1-106 (6), C.R.S., or any employee thereof engaged in his or her official employment duties, that sells large-capacity magazines exclusively to:

(I) A branch of the armed forces of the United States;

(II) A department, agency, or political subdivision of the state of Colorado, or of any other state, or of the United States government;

(III) A firearms retailer for the purpose of firearms sales conducted outside the state;

(IV) A foreign national government that has been approved for such transfers by the United States government; or

(V) An out-of-state transferee who may legally possess a large-capacity magazine; or

(b) An employee of any of the following agencies who bears a firearm in the course of his or her official duties:

(I) A branch of the armed forces of the United States; or

(II) A department, agency, or political subdivision of the state of Colorado, or of any other state, or of the United States government; or

(c) A person who possesses the magazine for the sole purpose of transporting the magazine to an out-of-state entity on behalf of a manufacturer of large-capacity magazines within Colorado.

33-6-125. Possession of a loaded firearm in a motor vehicle.

It is unlawful for any person, except a person authorized by law or by the division, to possess or have under his control any firearm, other than a pistol or revolver, in or on any motor vehicle unless the chamber of such firearm is unloaded. Any person in possession or in control of a rifle or shotgun in a motor vehicle shall allow any peace officer, as defined in section 33-1-102 (32), who is empowered and acting under the authority granted in section 33-6-101 to enforce articles 1 to 6 of this title to inspect the chamber of any rifle or shotgun in the motor vehicle. For the purposes of this section, a "muzzle-loader" shall be considered unloaded if it is not primed, and, for such purpose, "primed" means having a percussion cap on the nipple or flint in the striker and powder in the flash pan. Any person who violates this section is guilty of a misdemeanor and, upon conviction thereof, shall be punished by a fine of fifty dollars and an assessment of fifteen license suspension points.

Personal Protective Equipment for the Range

Eye and ear protection is required anytime you fire on the range. When you get your personal protection equipment, I recommend you purchase the highest quality you can; cheap protection will often fail when it is most inconvenient or dangerous. Your eyesight and hearing are far too valuable to risk with substandard equipment.

Eye protection: Glasses that cover the entire optical socket and a hat with a brim (baseball cap, etc.). There are many types of glasses on the market so price should not be your only determining factor. There are many good quality shooting glasses starting around $10.00 and going up from there. You do not need to get Oakley® or Gargoyles® that cost up to $150.00, however keep in mind these do provide good protection. What is important is the amount of protection the glasses provide you. The lens should be made of lexon or a similar impact resistant material that has an ANSI rating. Your cap brim should be large enough to prevent hot brass from getting behind your shooting glasses.

Ear protection: Earmuffs should have at least an ANSI rating of 21dbm. Just as with your shooting glasses, you don't need the highest priced set on the market. There are many good headsets starting around $20.00.

If you start shooting a lot or begin shooting in competition, you may, however, want to get electronic earmuffs ($150.00+). This type of hearing protection uses an electronic system to allow you to hear range commands or have conversations without having to yell, but blocks harmful noise. I wear electronic muffs in conjunction with the cheap, disposable foam plugs; the earmuffs amplify speech and other non-harmful sounds while both protect from the loud noise associated with shooting.

If you do not shoot often (less than 3 or 4 times per year) you can get good protection from earplugs, if they fit properly. The cheap foam plugs help, but do not provide sufficient protection by themselves for exposure to the repeated noise of gunfire. It is recommended you use both earplugs and earmuffs to better protect your hearing.

Other Range Equipment

In addition to the above listed safety equipment, there is some other equipment that should accompany you any time you go to the range. Depending on where and the time of year, some items need to be added or may be left out. I recommend these items be put in a range bag that can be left packed and includes all of your safety gear along with the following:

1. Water (at least one quart in summer or winter — more important during winter)
2. Sunscreen
3. Stapler/Tape/Targets
4. First Aid Kit (Hopefully never needed)
5. Cell Phone
6. Small tool kit (sight adjustment, etc.)
7. Cleaning Kit

Range Commands

The following is a list of basic range commands you will hear on the range. This is not a comprehensive list of commands, just the basic commands commonly used on most ranges.

Load and Make Ready: This is your time to insure your weapon is in the proper configuration for the next drill.

Unload and Clear: At this command, place your weapon on safe, remove the magazine, or open the cylinder, remove any ammunition in the weapon then visually and physically insure there is no ammunition present in your weapon before holstering.

Cease Fire: At this command, **STOP,** remove your finger from the trigger and stand by for instructions. DO NOT CHANGE YOUR POSITION TO FACE MORE DOWN RANGE. Anyone on the range can call a CEASE FIRE any time an unsafe condition is detected.

Range is going HOT: This is the warning to put on your eye and ear protection and insure you are not in front of the firing line.

Range is CLEAR: This command is given after all weapons have been cleared and or holstered. At this command you may remove your hearing and eye protection. Caution: if there is shooters are firing on adjacent bays you should leave your eye protection in place at a minimum.

About the Author

Born to a military family in France Timothy grew up in Hawaii and south Texas. His father, an avid marksman, started Tim shooting at a young age. He has been active in numerous shooting sports throughout his life.

He joined the USAF in 1984. He was trained in military weapons and secure communications equipment. He transitioned from the active duty Air Force to the Colorado National Guard for 6 years before transferring to the Colorado Air National Guard where his primary duty was as a weapons' instructor. He retired from the Colorado Air National Guard with 25 years total service. Since retiring from the service he has worked as a security guard for both private and military organizations and as a Deputy Sherriff

He currently works in corrections and is a lead firearms for the Sheriff's Office. He has served on the board of directors for the Front Range International Defensive Pistol Association for the past since 1997. He is a POST full skills instructor teaching handguns, shotguns and rifles. He is also a member of the Colorado Law Enforcement Firearms Instructors Association, the International Association of Firearms Instructors, and a life member of the NRA.

www.ingramcontent.com/pod-product-compliance
Lightning Source LLC
Chambersburg PA
CBHW042312150426
43199CB00005B/30